DISTURBING
Complacency

DISTURBING Complacency

Preparing for Christmas

Lisa Bodenheim

WILD GOOSE PUBLICATIONS

ISBN 978-1-905010-37-0

Cover illustration © 2007 Linda Schmidt

The publishers gratefully acknowledge the support of the Drummond Trust,
3 Pitt Terrace, Stirling FK8 2EY in producing this book.

A catalogue record for this book is available from the British Library.

Overseas distribution
Australia & New Zealand: Willow Connection Pty Ltd, Unit 4A, 3–9 Kenneth Road, Manly Vale, NSW 2093
New Zealand: Pleroma, Higginson Street, Otane 4170, Central Hawkes Bay
Canada: Novalis/Bayard, 10 Lower Spadina Ave., Suite 400, Toronto, Ontario M5V 2Z

Printed by Bell & Bain, Thornliebank, Glasgow

CONTENTS

Each day of the week has a theme:

Sunday	Spirit
Monday	Creation
Tuesday	Bible
Wednesday	Money
Thursday	Nation
Friday	Jesus
Saturday	Resistance

Acknowledgements

I give thanks to my parents, children, friends, and extended family. I also give thanks to parishioners, colleagues in parish ministry, professors and writers. Through them I have found a God both within and beyond church and they have provoked thoughts and feelings that have stimulated my faith so that it remains lively and growing.

Most especially, I give thanks to people, on both sides of the Atlantic who nurtured, critiqued, asked or answered questions and refined this project into the book that you now hold in your hands: Mary Beth Scow, Manda Stack, Linda McDonald, Yvonne Naylor, Hilary Marshall, Jo Salwey, Linda Schmidt, the authors who have given me persmission to quote their works and the staff of Wild Goose Publications.

A note about Advent

Advent, the season before Christmas, begins four Sundays before Christmas Day. The length of Advent varies depending on which day is December 25. This book can be used any year but not all passages of the fourth week will always be needed as it is set for the longest Advent, which is when December 25 falls on a Sunday.

Do you think a little water
        on your snakeskins
                is going to make any difference?

It's your life that must change,
        not your skin!

And don't think you can pull rank by claiming Abraham as your father.
Being a descendant of Abraham is neither here nor there.
Descendants of Abraham are a dime a dozen.

What counts is your life.
        Is it green and blossoming?

Because if it's deadwood,
        it goes on the fire.

Matthew 3:8–10
The MESSAGE: The Bible in Contemporary Language
by Eugene Peterson

INTRODUCTION

The Jewish religious leaders thought their nation was special because of their ancestor Abraham. Does living in an 'advanced' nation give us a similarly puffed-up view of our importance in God's eyes? Try substituting your country's name for the references to Abraham in those words of John the Baptist.

> 'And don't think you can pull rank by claiming the UK or US as your nation. Being a citizen of the UK or US is neither here nor there. Citizens of your nation are a dime a dozen.'

Living in a world of plenty, we are falling asleep spiritually. Many western Christians would prefer to push aside that saying from Jesus: 'Indeed, it is easier for a camel to go through the eye of a needle than for someone who is rich to enter the kingdom of God.' (Luke 18:25) We would claim that we are not really wealthy. But we fool only ourselves. If we embrace the plenty and refuse to acknowledge the poverty and violence that exist, we can rightly be accused of being 'deadwood'.

Let us prepare for the birth of Christ by stretching our faith and disturbing our comfort. Let us ruffle our complacency and develop awareness, a courageous spirit and a security that comes from a deep-rooted faith. Through our desire to know God more intimately, may we find the life that is 'green and blossoming'.

In this book you will find readings reflecting on the themes for each week and each day of Advent. If we allow time for quietness and space to sit with our own reflections, our hearts and minds will open wide and perhaps we will behold a different image of God. For it is when we become vulnerable that God can shape us.

FIRST WEEK
OF ADVENT

UNVEILED

If we wish to understand
the Old Testament word
  ruach
we must forget the word
  'spirit'
which belongs to Western culture.
The Greek word pneuma, *the Latin* spiritus,
and the Germanic Geist/ghost
were always conceived as antitheses
to matter and body.
They mean something immaterial …
But if we talk in Hebrew about Yahweh's ruach,
we are saying:

  God is a tempest,
    a storm,
      a force in body and soul,
        humanity and nature.

The Spirit of Life
A Universal Affirmation
by Jurgen Moltmann[1]

In the beginning when God created
the heavens and the earth,

the earth was a formless void
and darkness covered the face of the deep,

while a [ruach] *from God*
swept over the face of the waters.

Genesis 1:1–3

12

We are used to separating spirit from body. We even learn to place more value on spirit, for we consider it – rather than the body – as our gift from God. Yet, when we look at the original meaning of spirit from the Bible, we find that spirit and body belong together.

Moltmann writes more: 'Ruach *was probably originally an onomatopoeic word for a gale – for example, the strong wind which divided the Reed Sea for Israel's Exodus from Egypt (Ex. 14.21). The word always means something living compared with something dead, something moving, over against what is rigid and petrified. In the transferred sense, when the word is applied to God, the tempest becomes a parable for the irresistible force of the Creator's power, God's killing wrath and life-giving mercy (cf. Ezek 13.13f.; 36.26f.).*

'Because people saw the livingness of life in the inhaling and exhaling of air, ruach *was also the breath of life and the power to live enjoyed by human beings and animals …*

'The term is probably related to rewah = breadth. Ruach *creates space. It sets in motion. It leads out of narrow places into wide vistas, thus conferring life.'2

'Spirit' lacks energy and power compared to the richness and depth of *ruach*. Jesus, too, emphasised the importance of the body. In the prayer he taught, we are to ask God first for our daily bread to feed our bodies. After we take care of our physical needs, then we are to take care of our spirit by asking for forgiveness and forgiving others. We need to nurture both body and spirit.

'*Our Father in heaven, hallowed be your name. Your kingdom come. Your will be done, on earth as it is in heaven. Give us this day our daily bread. And forgive us our debts, as we also have forgiven our debtors.*' (Matthew 6:9–12)

'*Father, hallowed be your name. Your kingdom come. Give us each day our daily bread. And forgive us our sins, for we ourselves forgive everyone indebted to us.*' (Luke 11:2–4)

When did we start splitting body from spirit? After Jesus died and the Romans destroyed the Temple of Jerusalem, the Jewish faith went through difficult times. One of the outcomes of that era was the forced choice of being either Jew or Christian. No longer could a person be both.

As Christianity developed separately from Judaism, we kept the Jewish belief in one God. We kept their Hebrew scriptures but modified them by adding the New Testament and incorporating ancient Greek thought. It is from the Greek philosophers that Christians learned to separate body and spirit, and to value the spirit but not the body. Being human, consisting of both body and spirit, was broken. We did not notice this successful foreign graft imposed on what God created.

Through this tear in the fabric of human life, we learned to affirm the spirit but not the body. We stepped away from the biblical definition of spirit found in the Hebrew scriptures, away from the teachings of Jesus about caring for both body and spirit. Without realising it, we embraced a narrow, superficial vision of God's gift to us.

[The hymns of St. Patrick of Ireland]
draw our attention not simply to the goodness
of what has been created
but to a perception that within creation
there is something of the presence of the uncreated,
that is, God.
We need to ask
what it is about an emphasis on
the spiritual being within the material
that has so often frightened
Western traditions of spirituality,
to the point that, although words like these are attributed to
a saint of the Western Church,
they are in fact omitted
from versions of the hymn in many hymn-books
and in others treated merely as optional.

Listening for the Heartbeat of God
A Celtic Spirituality
by J. Philip Newell[3]

14

Then the Lord answered Job out of the whirlwind:

'Has the rain a father, or who has begotten the drops of dew?
From whose womb did the ice come forth,
and who has given birth to the hoarfrost of heaven?
The waters become hard like stone,
and the face of the deep is frozen.

Can you bind the chains of the Pleiades,

or loose the cord of Orion?

Can you lead forth the Mazzaroth in their season,

or can you guide the Bear with its children?

Do you know the ordinances of the heavens?

Can you establish their rule on the earth?

Can you lift up your voice to the clouds so that a flood of

waters may cover you?

Can you send forth lightnings, so that they may go and

say to you, 'Here we are'?

Who has put wisdom in the inward parts,

or given understanding to the mind?

Who has the wisdom to number the clouds?

Or who can tilt the waterskins of the heavens,

when the dust runs into a mass and the

clods cling together?

Job 38:1, 28–38

By praising only the spirit and not the body, we developed habits, through the centuries, intended to conquer the needs of the flesh. In like manner, we attempted to subdue creation. We stripped mountains to mine gems and minerals, cut down rainforests to graze cattle or make lumber, and dammed rivers for irrigation or transportation. As a result, we now have pollution, climate change, global warming, rapid extinction of animal life, decreased variety of plant life, and an increase in asthma and cancer among humankind.

Scientists report these facts. Some of our government leaders take these reports to heart; others ignore or challenge the studies. In churches, people of faith speak out increasingly about our need to care for the environment. As a result, many people are changing lifestyles.

We often use the first creation story to support our desire to control creation. *'God blessed* [humankind] *and God said "Be fruitful and multiply, and fill the earth and subdue it; and have dominion over the fish of the sea and over the birds of the air and over every living thing that moves upon the earth."'* (Genesis 1:28). It is a mistake to take this passage out of its place in the Bible. After five days of bringing forth all the rest of creation, God made humankind in God's image! Isn't there a suggestion here that we will continue to create and to preserve the diversity God has begun, and to praise its goodness?

This seems to be verified in the second creation story, *'The Lord God took the man and put him in the Garden of Eden to till it and keep it.'* (Genesis 2:15). If this sentence were more closely translated from the original Hebrew language, the phrase *'till it and keep it'* would instead read *'serve it and preserve it'*.[4]

Not all Christians grew up with the split between spirit and body. In Britain and Ireland, 'Celtic' spirituality evolved along a different path.

In the early third century, the Roman Empire colonised southern Britain, bringing Christianity with it. St Patrick took the new faith to Ireland. In the early fourth century, when the Germanic peoples invaded the Roman Empire on the continent of Europe, Rome left Britain to defend itself.

Christianity flourished in the British Isles. Attentive to the full creation stories, Celtic Christianity grew without the restrictions of the spirit/body split. Irish and Scottish prayers wove together spirit and earth. Celtic Christians practised *'listening to the heartbeat of God'* by being attentive to the presence of God within creation, by looking within their hearts. Male and female leaders established religious communities. Outdoor Celtic crosses, with their carvings teaching the faith, marked sacred sites.

Two hundred years after they had left, the Romans came back to Britain, re-establishing church structures and traditions. The authorities and the people who practised Roman Christianity discredited and eventually persecuted Celtic Christians.

Why devalue creation and body? Why did we so eagerly accept that the body and creation were there for us to conquer and subdue? Was there a desire for control over some part of our life apart from God's influence? Or was there a fear that God is disempowered if any part of God's spirit lives within the flesh, within creation?

There is more to the Honda
than the technology of mechanics.
And there is more to the Bible
than the technology of print.

Surrounding the machine technology of the Honda
there is a world of gravity and inertia, values and velocity,
surfaces and obstructions, traffic regulations and the police,
other drivers, snow and ice and rain.

There is far more to driving a car
than turning a key in the ignition
and stepping on the accelerator.
Those who don't know that are soon dead or maimed.

And those who don't know the world of the Bible
are likewise dangerous
to themselves and others.

Living the Message
Daily Reflections
by Eugene Peterson [5]

The two angels arrived at Sodom in the evening. Lot was sitting at the city gate. He saw them and got up to welcome them, bowing before them and said, 'Please, my friends, come to my house and stay the night. Wash up. You can rise early and be on your way refreshed.'

They said, 'No, we'll sleep in the street.'

But [Lot] insisted, wouldn't take no for an answer; and they relented and went home with him. Lot fixed a hot meal for them and they ate.

Before they went to bed men from all over the city of Sodom, young and old, descended on the house from all sides and boxed them in. They yelled to Lot, 'Where are the men who are staying with you for the night? Bring them out so we can have our sport with them!'

Lot went out, barring the door behind him and said, 'Brothers, please, don't be vile! Look, I have two daughters, virgins; let me bring them out; you can take your pleasure with them, but don't touch these men – they're my guests.'

They said, 'Get lost! You drop in from nowhere and now you're going to tell us how to run our lives. We'll treat you worse than them!' And they charged past Lot to break down the door.

18

But the two men reached out and pulled Lot inside the house, locking the door. Then they struck blind the men who were trying to break down the door, both leaders and followers, leaving them groping in the dark.

The two men said to Lot, 'Do you have any other family here? Sons, daughters – anybody in the city? Get them out of here, and now! We're going to destroy this place. The outcries of victims here to God are deafening; we've been sent to blast this place into oblivion.'

Genesis 19:1–13

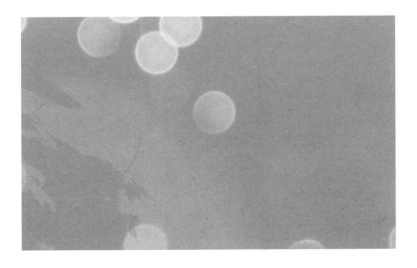

This biblical story is often used to point to God's condemnation of homosexual behaviour. We read the Bible through the Western eyes of our 21st-century world. The ancient Israelite people heard this story through the Eastern ears of their 17th-century world – BC.

We live in an information- and communication-based culture that relies heavily on electronic equipment and technology: phones, mobile phones, computers, laptops, iPods, and Palm Pilots. We use fossil fuel for transportation: cars, boats, motorcycles, trains and planes. We live in houses connected to an electrical matrix that keeps us warm or cool at the push of a button. We cook our food at the turn of a dial.

The ancient Israelites lived in an agricultural and crafts-based peasant culture. They relied heavily on their memories to pass on stories and traditions. They used their feet, their arms, the wind or animals for transportation. They added or removed the cloth walls of their homes and the clothing of their body to keep warm or cool. They cooked over fires.

Do we truly let this story of the Bible speak to us? Or do we interpret it from our perspective? Sodom and Gomorrah had an important lesson for the early Israelite people to pass on to later generations. It is a story of God's judgement. What does God condemn, as seen from the perspective of the ancient Israelite?

The prophet Ezekiel, who lived in the 5th century BC, wrote, *'This was the guilt of your sister Sodom: she and her daughters*

19

had pride, excess of food, and prosperous ease, but did not aid the poor and needy.' (Ezekiel 16:49)

Jesus mentions Sodom and Gomorrah in Matthew 10 as he delegates the power to heal and gives instructions to his disciples. Then Jesus sends them off to various cities and villages. *'If anyone will not welcome you or listen to your words, shake off the dust from your feet as you leave that house or town. Truly I tell you, it will be more tolerable for the land of Sodom and Gomorrah on the day of judgement than for that town.'* (Matthew 10:14–15)

What was Jesus referring to? Was he talking about sexual orientation? Jesus has told the disciples in the previous verse to knock on doors, be courteous in their greeting, gentle in conversation if the people welcome them. If the people do not welcome them, the disciples are to shake off the dust from their feet as they leave. Jesus is not referring to sex. He is referring to acceptance, receptiveness and hospitality.

It is difficult for us to understand the stories of Genesis from a hospitality-oriented 17th-century-BC point of view. We live in a sexually vigilant 21st-century-AD culture. Sexuality and hospitality are wedded together in this story. The angels prevented the gang rape of themselves, as men, as well as of Lot's two daughters. One of the foundations of ancient Israelite culture was hospitality to the stranger and sojourner. The threat of violence, sexual or not, went against their culture.

The common thread weaving these stories together is hospitality. Hospitality is courteous. Hospitality welcomes and listens. The opposite of hospitality is not homosexuality. The opposite of hospitality is intolerance, hostility, violence. From the ancient Israelite perspective, God condemned this lack of hospitality in Sodom and Gomorrah.

Imagine a [United Kingdom] football match
between Manchester United
and your local primary school team.
Not hard to guess who would win.
Then imagine that the school team had to play
in oversized boots,
on a field sloping downhill towards their goal
and with only Manchester United supporters allowed to attend.

Slightly surreal?

This is, however,
akin to the ludicrous state
of world trade rules.

Finding a Place in the World
by Abi Sampson [6]

[King] David dispatched Joab and his fighting men of Israel in full force to destroy the Ammonites for good. They laid siege to Rabbah, but David stayed in Jerusalem.

One late afternoon, David got up from taking his nap and was strolling on the roof of the palace. From his vantage point on the roof he saw a woman bathing. The woman was stunningly beautiful. David sent to ask about her, and was told, 'Isn't this Bathsheba, daughter of Eliam and wife of Uriah the Hittite?' David sent his agents to get her. After she arrived, he went to bed with her. (This occurred during the time of 'purification' following her period.) Then she returned home. Before long she realised she was pregnant.

22

Later she sent word to David: 'I'm pregnant.'

David then got in touch with Joab: 'Send Uriah the Hittite to me.' Joab sent him. When [Uriah] arrived, David asked him for news from the front – how things were going with Joab and the troops and with the fighting. Then he said to Uriah, 'Go home. Have a refreshing bath and a good night's rest.'

After Uriah left the palace, an informant of the king was sent after him. But Uriah didn't go home. He slept that night at the palace entrance, along with the king's servants. David was told that Uriah had not gone home. He asked Uriah, 'Didn't you just come off a hard trip? So why didn't you go home?'

Uriah replied to David, 'The Chest is out there with the fighting men of Israel and Judah – in tents. My master Joab and his servants are roughing it out in the fields. So, how can I go home and eat and drink and enjoy my wife? On your life, I'll not do it!'

In the morning David wrote a letter to Joab and sent it with Uriah. In the letter he wrote, 'Put Uriah in the front lines where the fighting is the fiercest. Then pull back and leave him exposed so that he's sure to be killed.'

2 Samuel 11:1b–11, 14–15

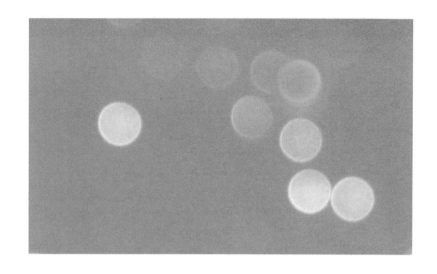

Abi Sampson continues, *'Trade Rules are made in the World Trade Organization (WTO). Rich countries can afford to employ hundreds of negotiators to champion their interests at WTO meetings. Some of the poorest countries aren't able to employ any. The result of this is unfair rules.'* [7]

The WTO is one of several agencies that are part of our global economic system. As of December 15, 2005, there were 149 countries classified as members of the WTO. Another 31 countries had observer status, negotiating to become full-fledged members. [8] The purpose of the WTO is *'to be a forum where all member countries can reach agreement on lowering tariffs (or taxes) on foreign trade.'* [9]

Economics frames people's relationship to money and work. Our current economic system, capitalism, promotes competition for resources and work within a free market structure. Characterised by private or corporate ownership, capitalism has existed for the past 500 years.

The more money we have, the more power we have. How shall we use our power? How should our governing bodies use power?

David abused his power. He had sex with Bathsheba while his men, including her husband, were fighting for his country. When Uriah, unknowingly, did not cooperate with David's attempt to cover his sin, David gave orders to ensure that Uriah would be killed. It was only after the prophet Nathan told the parable of the poor man's single lamb slaughtered by the rich man that David's eyes opened, in horror, to his sin and he repented.

As followers of Jesus, how shall we use money? Today's quote of the unevenly matched football game (soccer to US readers) is a parable that highlights abuse of power within the WTO. Will our eyes open to our sin? And if our eyes open, will we have the courage to repent? Will we have the openness and creativity to be part of changing the system?

How does Jesus use power? Through compassion, Jesus healed people, illustrated parables with images from nature, confronted religious authorities, and proclaimed that the Community of God was near. Does our economic system demonstrate compassion toward people, use nature to point to God's generosity, or bring us closer to the Community of God? It does not.

'The business of the WTO should be of interest to us because the rules that are being decided therein have an impact on our country, its economy, inhabitants, and everything that has to do with our lives, what we eat, how we dress, what we buy and sell.' [10]

Since economics is a human-created tool it is to be subservient to our faith in God. If our governing leaders conveniently close their eyes to the sin of becoming subservient to our economic system, then as citizens we may need to shake and rattle a few gold-encrusted ivory towers.

There are few rhetorical inhibitions these days
when it comes to extolling our own virtues
and drawing attention to someone else's vices.
But there is another attitude
that is even more threatening.
It implies that criticism of one's own country
(or one's own point of view, or one's own church)
is hitting below the belt
and therefore against the rules.

26

To criticise,
particularly in a public way,
is to weaken the cause of those criticised;
it thus becomes an act of disloyalty
that gives aid and comfort to the enemy.

Unexpected News:
Reading the Bible with Third World Eyes
by Robert McAfee Brown [11]

[Jesus] came to Nazareth where he had been reared. As he always
did on the Sabbath, he went to the meeting place. When he stood
up to read, he was handed the scroll of the prophet Isaiah.
Unrolling the scroll, he found the place where it was written,
'God's Spirit is on me, he's chosen me to preach the message of
good news to the poor, sent me to announce pardon to prisoners
and recovery of sight to the blind, to set the burdened and battered
free, to announce,
'This is God's year to act!'

He rolled up the scroll, handed it back to the assistant, and sat down. Every eye in the place was on him, intent. Then [Jesus] started in, 'You've just heard Scripture make history. It came true just now in this place.'

All who were there, watching and listening, were surprised at how well [Jesus] spoke. But they also said, 'Isn't this Joseph's son, the one we've known since he was a youngster?'

He answered, 'I suppose you're going to quote the proverb, "Doctor, go heal yourself. Do here in your hometown what we heard you did in Capernaum." Well, let me tell you something: No prophet is ever welcomed in his hometown. Isn't it a fact that there were many widows in Israel at the time of Elijah during that three and a half years of drought when famine devastated the land, but the only widow to whom Elijah was sent was in Sarepta in Sidon? And there were many lepers in Israel at the time of the prophet Elisha but the only one cleansed was Naaman the Syrian.'

That set everyone in the meeting place seething with anger. They threw him out, banishing him from the village, then took him to a mountain cliff at the edge of the village to throw him to his doom but he gave them the slip and was on his way.

Luke 4:16–30

Is it disloyal to critique our government, our institutions or our structures? Does democracy require unswerving loyalty and trust, with no attempt to analyse or comment on the actions of our CEOs of institutions or our government leaders?

What is a democracy? It is defined as *'government in which the supreme power is vested in the people and exercised by them or their elected agents,' 'political or social equality'*, and *'the absence of hereditary or arbitrary class distinctions or privileges'*.

If we are not allowed to review, analyse or comment on those who are our CEOs or leaders, then we no longer have a demo-cracy. We have a dictatorship. It does not matter if we elect government leaders for limited terms. That freedom is an extremely limited democracy. It is just paying lip service to democracy if, once our leaders are elected, we are not allowed to critique their actions.

As Christians, we have inherited a tradition that asks us to learn, reflect and act. That is what Jesus did. He learned the tradi-tions of Judaism — the stories, the laws and the prophets. He took time to develop a relationship with God through prayer. Then he applied God's gift of intelligence to review, critique and analyse the traditions of his faith to see if they were still in alignment with God's will.

Jesus saw deficiencies. Not surprising, since anything made by human hands or minds falls short of God's glory. We are finite and limited, whereas God is eternal and unlimited. As the quote from Luke shows, Jesus's public criticism was not well received. When the people were sceptical, Jesus pushed his analysis further. The people became angry, defensive, violent.

The Christian year is set up to encourage people of faith to review and reflect upon our traditions. We have two cycles in the Christian year: Advent, Christmas, Epiphany and the Sundays after Epiphany (also known as Ordinary Time) and Lent, Easter,

Pentecost and the Sundays after Pentecost (also known as Ordi-nary Time).

Our high holidays of celebration are Christmas and Easter. We approach Christmas and Easter by first living through Advent and Lent. Advent and Lent are times of warning and penitence, times of critical reflection of our faith life, both as individuals and as communities. During these times we make room for confessions. We drop our defensiveness. We acknowledge that we are not God. We confess that we are not the Creator of all that is. We are finite and fall short of the glory of God.

As 'advanced' nations, do we try to maintain an image of perfection? Do we have to be superior to other nations, playing 'king of the mountain'? There is much that is good in Europe, North America and Australasia but we are not infallible. Each nation has its problems. We each have our sins. We are not the Creator, are not God. It is good for us to remember that.

There was a radical social and political edge
to [Jesus's] message and activity.
He challenged the social order of his day
and indicted the elites who dominated it.
He had a clever tongue,
which could playfully or sarcastically
indict the powerful and proper.
He must have been remarkably courageous,
willing to continue what he was doing
even when it became clear
that it was putting him in lethal danger.

Meeting Jesus Again for the First Time
The Historical Jesus & The Heart of Contemporary Faith
by Marcus J. Borg [12]

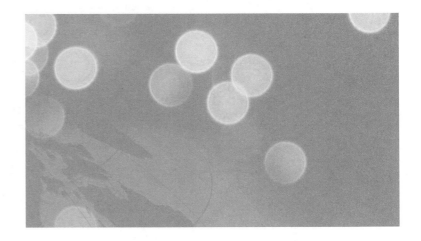

When the Passover Feast, celebrated each spring by the Jews, was about to take place, Jesus travelled up to Jerusalem. He found the Temple teeming with people selling cattle and sheep and doves. The loan sharks were also there in full strength.

Jesus put together a whip out of strips of leather and chased them out of the Temple, stampeding the sheep and cattle, upending the tables of the loan sharks, spilling coins left and right. He told the dove merchants, 'Get your things out of here! Stop turning my Father's house into a shopping mall!' That's when his disciples remembered the Scripture, 'Zeal for your house consumes me.'"

John 2:13–17

30

It almost feels as if, at the end of this scripture passage, we should raise our fist in the air, shouting, 'Go, Jesus.' We want to cheer him on for upsetting the status quo, for challenging structures that oppress his people and for shaking up the dominant elite.

Generally, we do this when we forget that Jesus was a Jewish man representing his people. We cheer Jesus on because we forget that we are the status quo, the dominant elite.

Our lifestyles rely on structures that oppress other people, even though we may feel that we do not have as much money as certain celebrities or politicians. Whether we want it or not, the majority of white citizens in the Western nations have power. In today's context, Jesus would be using his clever tongue on us.

The word 'power' comes from old French and Latin words meaning 'to be able'. Traditionally defined as might, strength, energy, the ability to act or produce an effect, power also means a person or a nation who has control or authority. Jesus lived during a time when the Roman Empire had political control and authority over the Jewish people, reinforced by military power.

'Abuse of power … is motivated by fear and by the resulting desire to control the power of life. This fear and arrogance are then used to create societies in which structures of domination create special possibilities for the privileged at the expense of shared power for all persons. The power that is intended by God for everyone who lives is used to destroy relationships in exchange for control. Rather than live in insecurity, some persons choose to create structures that dominate and control others for personal gratification and false security.' 13

The Romans seized and kept power through military force. The Sadducees, priests in the Temple of Jerusalem, gained power by cooperating with the Romans. Jesus's power and authority came from the inner Source of all power. From that Source of all life, Jesus redefined power.

Jesus chose not to use his power to assassinate or overthrow the Roman authority or their military presence. He chose to resist the structures that the religious authorities relied upon to keep their place of privilege, which placed a heavy burden on the outcast and marginalised. Jesus used his power to chastise, to confront and to challenge the people who benefited from abuse of power, whether they abused power consciously or not.

Abuse of power is motivated by fear or the attempt to control the power of life, which is contrary to our understanding of God. Fear constricts, restricts and narrows our vision. From the creation story in the book of Genesis, we learn of a God who values expansion, diversity and broad vistas. Only by letting go of fear does the power of life blossom.

Jesus shows us the God-centred way to use power: to own the power that belongs to us and to use that power well — not to assassinate or kill but to chastise, to confront, and to challenge the abuse of power that we will be able to see when we look through eyes of faith focused on the Community of God through Jesus.

Because illness
is a symbolic condition,
that is, a dislocation in the symbolic net that comprises society,
Jesus' actions are correspondingly symbolic …
Insofar as healing restores wholeness,
the meaning of health coincides
with one of the meanings of holiness.
By privileging the image of holiness-as-wholeness
over that of holiness-as-separation
it exposes the latter as a form of social mutilation.
By restoring health, as inclusion,
Jesus redesigns boundaries,
bringing in those who previously needed to be left out
for the society to succeed.

Nonviolent Story:
Narrative Conflict Resolution in the Gospel of Mark
by Robert R. Beck [14]

They came to the other side of the sea, to the country of the Gerasenes. And when [Jesus] had stepped out of the boat, immediately a man out of the tombs with an unclean spirit met him.

He lived among the tombs; and no one could restrain him anymore, even with a chain; for he had often been restrained with shackles and chains, but the chains he wrenched apart, and the shackles he broke in pieces; and no one had the strength to subdue him.

Night and day among the tombs and on the mountains he was always howling and bruising himself with stones. When he saw Jesus from a distance, he ran and bowed down before him; and he shouted at the top of his voice, 'What have you to do with me, Jesus, Son of the Most High God? I adjure you by God, do not torment me.' For [Jesus] had said to him, 'Come out of the man, you unclean spirit!'

Then Jesus asked him, 'What is your name?' He replied, 'My name is Legion; for we are many.' He begged [Jesus] earnestly not to send them out of the country. Now there on the hillside a great herd of swine was feeding; and the unclean spirits begged [Jesus], 'Send us into the swine; let us enter them.' So he gave them permission. And the unclean spirits came out and entered the swine; and the herd, numbering about two thousand, rushed

32

down the steep bank into the sea, and were drowned in the sea.

The swineherds ran off and told it in the city and in the country. Then people came to see what it was that had happened. They came to Jesus and saw the demoniac sitting there, clothed and in his right mind, the very man who had had the legion; and they were afraid. Those who had seen what had happened to the demoniac and to the swine reported it. Then they began to beg Jesus to leave their neighbourhood.

Mark 5:1–17

'Resistance' means to withstand, to strive against, the act of opposing a force, to prevent motion, to refrain or abstain from, to withstand the action of an effect. Jesus resisted certain teachings within his religious tradition. One of the teachings he resisted was holiness-as-separation.

Holiness-as-separation, defined in the book of Leviticus, values purity. Holiness-as-wholeness values healing, and for healing to occur, compassion is needed. In the Bible, the books of the Law emphasise purity and the books of the Prophets emphasise compassion.

The Gerasene demoniac was exiled from living in his community. He lived among the tombstones. He was not pure. He needed to be separated from his community. Jesus resisted the tidy definition of holiness-as-separation. Jesus healed and liberated the Gerasene demoniac, giving him new life, a new social status. The freed man took the position of a disciple, by sitting at Jesus's feet *'clothed and in his right mind'*.

The townspeople reacted with fear. Jesus subverted their tidy rules and doctrines about who belonged and who did not. If Jesus had the power to restore banished or exiled people into society, it would change lives. What would parents, husbands, wives, children and friends have to change to bring the outcast back into their homes? What relationship dynamics would have to be abandoned to make room for health and wholeness?

Change would be required if they were to use compassion rather than purity to define relationships. When the townspeople

33

begged Jesus to leave their neighbourhood, they were the ones, metaphorically speaking, who lived among the tombs.

Do we chain ourselves to tombs? Have we tied ourselves to a certain assumed perspective of the world that we refuse to change? When we read a magazine article or book that makes us uncomfortable, will we quit reading? When we listen to another person challenge our understanding of the world, either on television or face-to-face, will we switch the channel or plug our hearts?

Jesus came not to abolish the law and the prophets, but to fulfil them. There is a place for the law, for seeking purity, but Jesus showed us that love is not subject to the law. If we are disciples of Christ, we are called to subject purity to compassion. Healing our communities is more important than being concerned about our own holiness.

The choice is before us. Will we let our complacency chain us to tombs? Or will we have courage as we seek Jesus, the living Christ, to allow God's *ruach* to blow change into our lives, to heal our brokenness and restore our communities? The choice is always ours.

SECOND WEEK
OF ADVENT

FEAR

The shekinah

is manifest in the symbols
of cloud, fire, or radiant light
that descend, overshadow, or lead the people.

The form which comes to be associated most clearly with her
is divine glory or kabod,
the weighty radiance that flashes out in unexpected ways
in the midst of the broken world.

Most significant is her work of accompaniment,
for 'Wherever the righteous go, the Shekinah goes with them.'

No place is too hostile.
She accompanies the people through the post-slavery wilderness,
and hundreds of years later into exile again,
through all the byways of rough times.

She Who Is
The Mystery of God in Feminist Theological Discourse
by Elizabeth A. Johnson[1]

The Lord

went in front of them
in a pillar of cloud by day,
to lead them along the way,

and in a pillar of fire by night,
to give them light,
so that they might travel by day and by night.

Neither the pillar of cloud by day
nor the pillar of fire by night
left its place in front of the people.

Exodus 13:21–22

What is at stake if we can only refer to God as 'he' or 'He'? Do we believe certain body types have more God-like qualities than other body types? Many people address God as 'he' knowing that this is not adequate, yet definitely not wishing to use 'she' to refer to God. What are we afraid of?

There are many images of God in the Bible. In the first creation story, God states a command, the command is fulfilled, and then God pronounces it good. God is majestic and powerful.

'In Genesis 2, God shapes the body of man first, then of plants and animals, then God shapes woman, letting the man name all things. After this God walks with the man and woman in the Garden of Eden. God is intimate, familiar. One image is reserved and structured, more authoritarian; the other is warm and artistic, a God who collaborates in partnership.

Although it is difficult to tell from the English translation, two different images of God are placed next to each other in today's passage from Exodus by using the masculine word 'Lord' and the feminine image of accompaniment within the cloud and the fire. The images are kept together.

Jesus used many images of God. If we look at the number of times God is referred to as father, it increases in the later written gospels. In Mark, the first written gospel, Jesus referred to God as father four times. In John, the last written gospel, God is referred to as father 109 times. As the days of Jesus's life, death and resurrection became more distant, the patriarchal culture of that time shaped the gospel writers' memories. When the memories were finally put into written form, they were not just factual accounts of what actually happened but were influenced by the writer's life as well.

The biblical images we have of God may seem to be opposites, yet ancient people of faith did not choose one image over the other. They chose both. Do we honestly think we have the capability to define fully who God is? What happens when we only allow one image of the sacred?

In her book, Johnson writes *So we may ask again Elie Wiesel's* [a Jewish survivor of the holocaust] *terrifying question [Where is God?]. When a woman is raped and murdered, what does the Shekinah say? She says, my body is heavy with violation. Through the long night when the Bethlehem concubine [Judges 19:25] is gang-raped and tortured, where is God? She is there, being abused and defiled. There too being burned to death by the Inquisition. There too being tortured by the male enforcers of unjust rule …*

There is no solution here, no attempt at theoretical reconciliation of atrocity with divine will. Only a terrible sense of the mystery of evil and the absence of God, which nevertheless may betray divine presence, desecrated.' [2]

Desecration of God happens when we devalue anything that God has created and pronounced good. Was the evil that happened then, and still happens today, caused by restricting God to one image? In today's English language, 'he' definitely refers to male, not generic, humankind. Do we not create idolatry if we can only refer to God in one image? Is it evil when we limit the mystery and awe of God?

You shall not make for yourself an idol, whether in the form of anything that is in heaven above, or that is on the earth beneath, or that is in the water under the earth.

Exodus 20:4

SECOND MONDAY OF ADVENT - CREATION

… nothing in nature is evil in itself.
That is, we and all creation bear within us,
however covered over it may be,
the essential goodness of God.
If we become evil,
we are acting contrary to our essential nature.
[John Scotus] Eriugena's spirituality led him
not to look away from life
but further within;
he believed that when we look within ourselves
and within all that exists,
we will find darknesses and evil
but, deeper still,
the goodness of God.

Listening for the Heartbeat of God
A Celtic Spirituality
by J. Philip Newell[3]

How long will the land mourn,
and the grass of every field wither?

For the wickedness of those who live in it
the animals and the birds are swept away

and because people said,
'[God] is blind to our ways.'

Many shepherds have destroyed my vineyard,
they have trampled down my portion,

they have made my pleasant portion
a desolate wilderness.

They have made it a desolation;
desolate, it mourns to me.

The whole land is made desolate
but no one lays it to heart.

Jeremiah 12:4, 10–11

38

It is an uncommon thought, that creation has within it the *'essential goodness of God'*. We have had a tendency to search for God out there somewhere in the sky, where we assume heaven and God's kingdom is. Traditionally we do not look for God nearby, especially in creation. That smacks too much of nature worship. 'That's not Christian' – or so we think.

Nevertheless, one of the names we call God is 'Creator'. In Genesis 1 and 2 God created all that exists: the entire cosmos. Several times, after a day of creating, the phrase *'And God saw that it was good'* ends the day. We are caretakers of creation. We do not own it. In the Psalms we read, *'I am God, your God. For every wild animal of the forest is mine, the cattle on a thousand hills. I know all the birds of the air, and all that moves in the field is mine. If I were hungry, I would not tell you, for the world and all that is in it is mine.'* (Psalm 50:7b, 10–12).

Do we believe that human-made walls, stained-glass windows and a tall ceiling are what make a space sacred? Cannot a grove of pine trees with their many 'spires' also be a place where God is present?

We behave as though creation is a force that needs to be conquered and tamed. We create large, single-species factory farms with thousands of cows deep in mud, or pigs on concrete floors, or chickens kept in individual cages. We uproot windbreaks to create bigger fields. We plant large areas with a single species of corn, soybean or grain, generously applying chemicals to eliminate both benevolent and malevolent plants and insects.

When we stress uniformity and the need to control, we endanger God's gift of abundance, diversity and structure.

John Scotus Eriugena, a 9th-century Irish philosopher, served a school in France. Newell writes more, *'To know the Creator, we need only look at the things he has created. The way to learn about God, Eriugena believed, is "through the letters of Scripture and through the species of creation". He urges us to listen to these expressions of God and to "conceive of their meaning in our souls".'* [4] This is different from stating that God exists totally within creation. God's mystery is never fully contained within that which God created, yet creation can point us to God.

Do we listen for God through creation any more? Do we enjoy nature just for its own sake rather than for the money that logging that tree will bring? How is it that we have this desire for a perfect, green lawn with no dandelions, mowed in a precise manner? We have not always served or preserved creation as God has called us to do.

If we refuse to listen to what is happening to creation, for the sake of keeping our comfortable lifestyle, how will our nation face God? When we die and God asks 'Why is the water I created not drinkable?' or 'Why are there only four different types of apple trees when I created a huge variety?' how will we respond?

The world was created by God, for God's glory.

You shall not murder.
Exodus 20:13

The simple act of buying a Bible
has subtle side effects we need to counter.

It is easy to suppose that since
we bought it,
we own it,
and therefore we can use it

the way we wish.

Living The Message
Daily Reflections
by Eugene Peterson [5]

As [Jesus] was setting out on a journey, a man ran up to him
and knelt before him, and asked him,
'Good Teacher, what must I do to inherit eternal life?'

Jesus said to him,
'Why do you call me good? No one is good but God alone.
You know the commandments:
"You shall not murder,
You shall not commit adultery;
You shall not steal:
You shall not bear false witness;
You shall not defraud;
Honuor your father and mother."'

He said to [Jesus],
'Teacher, I have kept all these since my youth.'

Jesus, looking at him, loved him and said,
'You lack one thing; go, sell what you own,
and give the money to the poor,
and you will have treasure in heaven;
then come, follow me.'

When he heard this, he was shocked and went away grieving, for he had many possessions. Then Jesus looked around and said to his disciples,

'How hard it will be for those who have wealth to enter the kingdom of God!'

Mark 10:17–23

If we buy a Bible and call it 'mine', we claim ownership. When we own something, we believe we have the right to use it as we wish. How do we use the Bible when we call it 'mine'? It is easy to pick our favourite phrases here and there, using them to justify our attitude and behaviour. Do we use the Bible as a weapon or as good news?

Many things have been justified through the Bible: slavery, a husband's right to abuse his wife, parents' rights to abuse their children, doctors' and pharmacists' refusal of birth control to women, family members refusing medical treatment for diabetes or mental illness, and condemnation of homosexuality.

Perhaps, as with the rich young man in the Bible, we ignore the parts of the Bible we don't like. He ignored the prophets, who urged people with power and money to consider the widow, the orphan and the refugee. The rich young man valued his money and comfort more than he valued his neighbour.

In Matthew 22:37–41 '[Jesus] *said* [to the lawyer], *"'You shall love the Lord your God with all your heart and with all your soul, and with all your mind.' This is the greatest and first commandment. And a second is like it: 'You shall love your neighbour as yourself.' On these two commandments hang all the law and the prophets."* Jesus reworded the commandments, showing us how fluid the scriptures were. Scriptures were an oral tradition long before they were written words. This does not invalidate the sacredness of the Bible, but we need to consider this as we interpret it. Here Jesus emphasised love for one's neighbour as being as important as love for God.

41

Again, Jesus talks about love of neighbour in this passage, *'Then Jesus said to the crowds and to his disciples, "The scribes and the Pharisees sit on Moses' seat; therefore, do whatever they teach you and follow it; but do not do as they do, for they do not practise what they teach. They tie up heavy burdens, hard to bear, and lay them on the shoulders of others; but they themselves are unwilling to lift a finger to move them."'* (Matthew 23:1–4)

Do we use the Bible to oppress and impoverish people? Does our faith cause us to contain and rigidly structure our lives and the lives of the people around us?

Or do we use the Bible to liberate and free people from poverty and violence? Does our faith open us up to fully express the goodness God has planted within us?

It is easy to assume that all we need to know about God, Jesus, the Holy Spirit and our faith lies between the covers of the Bible. Did God only speak to us in the past – in particular, the past recorded in the Bible? Does God no longer speak to us in the present or in the future? What happens when we allow the Bible, sacred though it is, to be God's only voice?

If the Bible does not point us toward God, but instead speaks for God, then the Bible has become our god.

I am the Lord your God, who brought you out of the land of Egypt, out of the house of slavery; you shall have no other gods before me.

Exodus 20:2

42

The story of Africa is particularly tragic.
Between 1960
(when many countries moved to independence)
and 1980,
sub-Saharan Africa's income per person grew by 36%.
Since 1980,
when structural adjustment policies started to bite,
their income has fallen by 13%.
The continent's share of world trade
is now only 2%,
and for sub-Saharan Africa
it is only 1.6%.
Without South Africa that figure falls to 1.2%.
This is a result of, not despite,
a decade or more of ruthless structural adjustment.

It Doesn't Have to Be Like This
Global Economics: A New Way Forward
by Margaret Legum [6]

Sitting across from the offering box, [Jesus] was observing how the crowd tossed money in for the collection. Many of the rich were making large contributions. One poor widow came up and put in two small coins – a measly two cents.

Jesus called his disciples over and said, 'The truth is that this poor widow gave more to the collection than all the others put together. All the others gave what they'll never miss; she gave extravagantly what she couldn't afford – she gave her all.'

Mark 12:41–44

Most of us live comfortable lifestyles in economically and technologically advanced nations. We are complacent about what we own, where we live, how we purchase. We see things on television or that our neighbours have and think, 'Oh, I'd like one of those too,' and buy it, no thought about it. This lack of consciousness of how our money affects other people anaesthetises our faith.

Global economics is complex but not beyond understanding. Since the 1970s, the world's economy has been dominated by 'neo-liberal' capitalism. Its institutions are the World Trade Organization, the World Bank and the International Monetary Fund (IMF). The World Bank and the IMF developed the *'structural adjustment'* programme for giving international loans.

A nation that is struggling financially needs to agree to go through a structural adjustment before the World Bank or the IMF will approve a loan. Structural adjustment changes a nation's economic structure. It does so by reducing the role of government – by allowing profit-making corporations to offer public services, by relaxing environmental laws, by not regulating investment from other nations, and by removing restrictions on the flow of other nations' products into the struggling nation.

Not all nations have gone through a structural adjustment in order to receive a loan. Legum writes, *'From the 1970s the US began to buy far more than it sold because it was not competitive with the*

low-wage economies of emerging markets. Its high living standards would have had to be drastically reduced to bring it back into balance. It would have needed a structural adjustment, along the lines of that which took place in Britain, to make it globally competitive. Indeed, had [the US] been a poor country seeking international finance, it would have been forced so to do.' [7]

The purpose of a structural adjustment is to make the country receiving the loan more competitive in the free market system and therefore able to pay back its loan. But the general result has been the loss of small or family-run businesses, fewer jobs, decreased wages, and environmental damage.

Legum shares the results for one nation that undertook a structural adjustment, *'"Why have you failed?" a World Bank expert asked Julius Nyerere, the former President of Tanzania, at a Washington meeting. He replied, "The British Empire left us a country with 85% illiterates, two engineers and 12 doctors. When I left office in 1985, we had 9% illiterates and thousands of engineers and doctors. At that point our income per capita was twice what it is today — after the Structural Adjustment programme. We now have one third less children in our schools, and public health and social services are in ruins. During those years, Tanzania has done everything that the World Bank and the IMF have demanded. So I ask you: Why have you failed?"'* [8]

Have our developed nations become like the rich in the Bible passage from the gospel of Mark, thinking we are benevo-

lent? Are poorer countries giving much more in relation to their poverty? Do we only give what we will not miss?

You shall not covet your neighbour's house; you shall not covet your neighbour's wife, or male or female slave, or ox, or donkey, or anything that belongs to your neighbour.

Exodus 20:17

The people who built the Tower of Babel
had only one language,
and their sole purpose was to prove to themselves
and to anyone else watching
how superior they were.
They did this by trying to demonstrate
that big was best,
building a monument to their own conceit to prove the point.
And God would not tolerate it.
When any building, any enterprise,
becomes an all-consuming passion,
it displaces God
and with God all those whom God shelters
– the poor, the weak, the marginalised.
In this light, we may see the history of civilisation
as a story of rival nations
struggling to become global powers
and enforcing uniformity on the world.

States of Bliss and Yearning
The Marks and Means of Authentic Christian Spirituality
by John L. Bell [9]

Now the whole earth had one language and the same words. And as they migrated from the east, they came upon a plain in the land of Shinar and settled there. And they said to one another,

'Come, let us make bricks, and burn them thoroughly.'

And they had brick for stone, and bitumen for mortar. Then they said,

'Come, let us build ourselves a city, and a tower with its top in the heavens, and let us make a name for ourselves; otherwise we shall be scattered abroad upon the face of the whole earth.'

The Lord came down to see the city and the tower, which mortals had built. And the Lord said,

'Look, they are one people, and they have all one language; and this is only the beginning of what they will do; nothing that they propose to do will now be impossible for them. Come, let us go down, and confuse their language there, so that they will not understand one another's speech.'

So the Lord scattered them abroad from there over the face of all the earth, and they left off building the city. Therefore it was called Babel, because there the Lord confused the language of all the earth; and from there the Lord scattered them abroad over the face of all the earth.

Genesis 11:1–9

48

What happens when we collapse the boundaries between religion and nation? What happens when we worship our nation's virtues as much as, if not more than, we worship God?

This story of Babel, often used to explain the presence of many languages in our world, also tells what happens when we frame national arrogance with our structures, thinking we can reach God by our own human efforts. We have chosen to ignore this uncomfortable aspect of God's response to a single nation's efforts to, as Bell wrote, *'build a monument to their own conceit'* and enforce *'uniformity on the world'*.

Looking closely at the story, we can see that underneath the conceit, underneath the arrogance, lies fear. What was their fear? They feared that they would be *'scattered abroad upon the face of the whole earth'*. Out of fear, they did not trust God's creation of a good world. Through fear, they sought security through fame and greatness. When a nation's values displace God's values, that nation has then stolen the rightful place belonging to God.

Religious nationalism is also a theme in the book of Jonah. God called Jonah, a Jewish man, to proclaim judgement against the wickedness of the people of Nineveh. Why would God want a Jewish prophet to proclaim judgement to people who were enemies of the Jews, thereby giving them a chance to repent and receive God's mercy? Jonah refused God's call and ran away.

How do our wealthy nations today respond to requests for mercy regarding loans from the IMF and the World Bank that the continents of Africa and South America are trying to cope with? Are we willing to show mercy? Or do we defer their requests so they will be forgotten, ignored?

How did God respond to Jonah's refusal to let the people of Nineveh have the chance to experience God's grace? Through a storm on the sea, God arranged for Jonah to spend three days in the belly of a whale. Jonah obeyed God's request the second time. The people of Nineveh did repent, God was merciful – and Jonah was angry. He sulked. Jonah did not want God's grace to extend beyond his own nation's borders. Through the mercy shown to a foreign nation, an enemy nation, God challenged Jonah's limited understanding of who God is.

Religious nationalism gives us a false sense of security by building us up as a nation and requiring us to conform as one people. It creates antagonism toward those from other nations, who are different from us. We then view people from other nations as competing with us for consumer goods, for environmental resources, even as rivals for God's favour.

The story of Babel and the story of Jonah challenge us today. If we believe our nation can rely on its own fame and strength for security, we have allowed fear to steal God's place in our hearts. These two stories shred any belief that our nation is the only one that has God's grace, that our understanding of God is the only way.

You shall not steal
Exodus 20:15

Why then does Jesus go to Jerusalem?
Not to step out a divinely pre-scripted ritual unto death.
True, he goes in response to a mandate from God.
But this mandate is not that Jesus die
but instead that he struggle
to overcome those who promote death,
who cultivate its structures,
whose allegiance to it is seen in their willingness to kill
when to their advantage.
Jesus is liquidated by the lieutenants of death,
but they do not, this narrative asserts, prevail.
And so, when we imagine
that the baptismal mandate of Jesus
demands his death
and requires him to march as if in procession upon Jerusalem
in order to die there,
we must understand we work against the grain
of the Gospel [of Mark].

Nonviolent Story
Narrative Conflict Resolution in the Gospel of Mark
by Robert R. Beck [10]

[Jesus] then began explaining things to them:
    'It is necessary that the Son of Man proceed to an ordeal of suffering, be tried and found guilty by the elders, high priests, and religion scholars, be killed, and after three days rise up alive.'
    He said this simply and clearly so they couldn't miss it.
    But Peter grabbed him in protest. Turning and seeing his disciples, wavering, wondering what to believe, Jesus confronted Peter.
    'Peter, get out of my way! Satan, get lost! You have no idea how God works.'
    Calling the crowd to join his disciples, [Jesus] said, 'Anyone who intends to come with me has to let me lead. You're not in the driver's seat; I am. Don't run from suffering; embrace it. Follow me and I'll show you how. Self-help is no help at all. Self-sacrifice is the way, my way, to saving yourself, your true self. What good would it do to get everything you want and lose you, the real you? What could you ever trade your soul for?'

Mark 8:31–37

50

As Christians, we profess Jesus as Lord and Saviour. This statement gives meaning to his crucifixion. Jesus died to save us from our sins – a very simple statement that is open to a variety of interpretations.

The traditional understanding for most Christians is that we needed Jesus sacrificed on the cross in order to be reconciled to God. Jesus was God incarnate and as God incarnate he had to die on the cross to pay for our sins.

What if we are wrong? Does God require killing in order to forgive our sins? God does not make any statement about the need for Jesus to die on a cross. Jesus himself did not say that he had to die for our sins. Jesus did say he would suffer and die.

Why was he going to suffer? As a prophet, able to read the signs of his time, Jesus could foresee what was coming to him. He lived in a tumultuous era, with the Jewish nation colonised by the Roman Empire. The Romans dealt with rebels by publicly crucifying them as a deterrent to future rebels. Appointed by the Roman Empire as Temple priests, the Sadducees' biggest concern was to keep the Jewish nation alive. The Pharisees' main concern was the proper interpretation of Moses' Law in order to live a holy life within a pagan empire.

Jesus was not worried about physical survival or purity of faith. He challenged practices allowed at the Temple. He called the Pharisees 'frauds' and 'snakes'. John the Baptist was arrested and had his head chopped off for challenging the government and religious leaders, calling them unsavory names. Jesus well understood the consequences of his behaviour.

What if it was not Jesus's crucifixion that saves us? What if it was the way he lived his life that saves us? He told parables. He hung out with the socially unacceptable and the impure, healed people, and taught that the Community of God is at hand. Is it possible that Jesus would want us to focus on his lifestyle because that is what gives meaning to his crucifixion? It is not his crucifixion that saves us from our sins. It is his lifestyle, which led to his crucifixion, that saves us.

As Beck writes, *'True, he goes in response to a mandate from God. But this mandate is not that Jesus die but instead that he struggle to overcome those who promote death, who cultivate its structures, whose allegiance to it is seen in their willingness to kill when to their advantage.'*

Through his lifestyle, Jesus showed us that God forgives us, that God's Community is near. For that, his disciples deserted him, the religious leaders condemned him to death and the Roman authorities killed him.

You shall not make wrongful use of the name of the Lord your God, for the Lord will not acquit anyone who misuses his name.

Exodus 20:7

In 1493 – one year after Columbus's first voyage to America –
the Pope apportioned the non-European world among
the most powerful nations of his own continent.
By the time Mercator completed his Atlas 100 years later,
European domination had spread across the world,
and Mercator's Atlas was the embodiment of
Europe's geographical conception of the world
in an age of colonialism.
Since then thousands of atlases have been published.
They differ in many respects from Mercator's,
but all have a common feature:
they focus on the industrialised countries.
The country and continent of origin are represented
at a larger scale than other countries and continents.
If, together with the age of colonialism,
the view of the world that underpinned it is to come to an end,
we need a new geography –
one that is based on the equal status of all peoples.

The Peters World Atlas
The Earth in its True Proportion
by Arno Peters [11]

When Haman saw for himself that Mordecai didn't bow down and kneel before him, he was outraged. Meanwhile, having learned that Mordecai was a Jew, Haman hated to waste his fury on just one Jew; he looked for a way to eliminate not just Mordecai but all Jews throughout the whole kingdom of Xerxes.

Haman then spoke with King Xerxes: 'There is an odd set of people scattered through the provinces of your kingdom who don't fit in. Their customs and ways are different from those of everybody else. Worse, they disregard the king's laws. They're an affront; the king shouldn't put up with them. If it please the king, let orders be given that they be destroyed. I'll pay for it myself. I'll deposit 375 tons of silver in the royal bank to finance the operation.'

The king slipped his signet ring from his hand and gave it to Haman son of Hammedatha the Agagite, archenemy of the Jews.

'Go ahead,' the king said to Haman. 'It's your money – do whatever you want with those people.'

Esther 3:5–6, 8–11

52

White people dominated not only through military force but also by implanting their traditions, their religion, their politics and their worldview in the lives of the people they conquered. 'Colonialism' strips a nation of people of their power, their autonomy, their worldview. The conquerors took it upon themselves to define the identity of the conquered people.

Many people assume the worldview of conquerors is historical fact. In ancient times, people assumed the earth was flat. In the time of Jesus, people believed the earth was the fixed centre of the universe with the planets revolving around the earth. Copernicus, in the 1400s, became unpopular when he wrote that the earth was not the centre of the universe. Galileo, who taught in the 1500s that the earth moved around the sun, was convicted of heresy by the Christian church.

Dominant people generally perceive themselves as being right and do not take kindly to their worldview being challenged. The challenge in today's reading is not only about land mass. It is about the incorrectness of the worldview of the conqueror, yet again.

Arno Peters, a German historian, created both the Peters World Map and the Peters Atlas. The maps represent countries according to their surface area. Politics and power have no place in the maps except for the governmental boundaries of a country. The maps are physically accurate.

Are the results different? South America is almost two times the size of Europe. Africa is almost two times the size of North America. China is more than four times larger than Greenland.

In the book of Esther, we have a story of Jewish exiles living in Persia in the 5th century BC. The Jews were not colonised very successfully according to this story. *'There is an odd set of people scattered through the provinces of your kingdom who don't fit in. Their customs and ways are different from those of everybody else.'* How did Haman respond to people who refused to be colonised? He got permission from the king to kill them.

How do we respond to people who refuse to blend in with our Westernised nations? Do we avoid eye contact with someone who has a different skin colour than ours or who wears clothing we consider odd? Do we respond to other people depending upon what colour their skin is?

Are we suspicious because of people's difference? If someone looks like a person from the Middle East, are they potential terrorists? If they are Muslim, do they receive full citizenship rights, as Christian citizens do?

Do those of us who are white Christian citizens think other people need to adopt our worldview? We easily become defensive when the falseness of our perspective is pointed out. Would we prefer to keep our prejudiced worldview or develop relationships with people from whom we can learn, therefore enriching our relationship with God?

You shall not bear false witness against your neighbour.

Exodus 20:16

THIRD WEEK
OF ADVENT

HONOUR

[Wisdom] is of feminine grammatical gender:
hokmah *in Hebrew,*
sophia *in Greek,*
sapientia *in Latin.*

While this does not in itself determine anything,
the biblical depiction of Wisdom is itself consistently female,
casting her as sister, mother, female beloved,
chef and hostess, preacher, judge,
liberator, establisher of justice,
and a myriad of other female roles
wherein she symbolises transcendent power
ordering and delighting in the world.

She pervades the world, both nature and human beings,
interacting with them all
to lure them along the right path to life.

She Who Is
The Mystery of God in Feminist Theological Discourse
by Elizabeth A. Johnson[1]

The Lord created me as the beginning of his work,
the first of his acts of long ago.

Ages ago I was set up at the first,
before the beginning of the earth.
When there were no depths
I was brought forth,
when there were no springs abounding with water.

56

Before the mountains had been shaped, before the hills,
I was brought forth –
when he had not yet made earth and fields,
or the world's first bits of soil.

When he established the heavens,
I was there,
when he drew a circle on the face of the deep,
when he made firm the skies above,
when he established the fountains of the deep,
when he assigned to the sea its limit,
so that the waters might not transgress his command,
when he marked out the foundations of the earth,
then I was beside him,
like a master worker;

and I was daily his delight,
rejoicing before him always,
rejoicing in his inhabited world
and delighting in the human race.

Proverbs 8:22–31

It is wonderful to read passages about female images of God to counteract the male image that bombards us in everything from public Christian music, to televangelists, to books, to scriptures written in the English language! There is a definite investment to keep the word 'he' in reference to God.

Our faith language continues to be shaped by ancient men, by word of mouth until finally written as the books of the Bible. It is their worldview which defines their experience of faith. In addition, some modern men and women, preferring the wonderfully familiar image of God as Father, continue to promote 'he' in reference to God.

It takes a lot of attentiveness, digging in scriptures and some knowledge of Greek and Hebrew to realise that God is much larger than we can possibly imagine. God is so very unknowable yet God creates our universe, blesses our world and loves us.

Wisdom is a common figure in scriptures. She can be found in the books of Job 28:20–28 and Proverbs, chapters 1, 8 and 9 and also in the books of Sirach, Baruch and Wisdom of Solomon. These last three books were cast out of the Bible during the Protestant Reformation in the 1500s. Some Bibles now have them listed in the Apocrypha, inserted between the Old and New Testaments.

Does the figure of wisdom have anything to do with Jesus? In the opening to the Gospel of John, can you see the similarities between the description of Jesus and the description of Wisdom in Proverbs? [8]

'In the beginning was the Word, and the Word was with God, and the Word was God. He was in the beginning with God. All things came into being through him, and without him not one thing came into being. What has come into being in him was life, and the life was the light of all people. The light shines in the darkness, and the darkness did not overcome it.'

(John 1:1–5)

This description of Wisdom from Sirach 51:26–27 *'Put your neck under [wisdom's] yoke, and let your souls receive instruction; it is to be found close by. See with your own eyes that I have laboured but little and found for myself much serenity'* is similar to Jesus's saying: *'Come to me all you that are weary and are carrying heavy burdens, and I will give you rest. Take my yoke upon you, and learn from me; for I am gentle and humble in heart, and you will find rest for your souls. For my yoke is easy and my burden is light.'* (Matthew 11:28–30)

There are connections between Jesus and wisdom. God is both he and she. Expanding our understanding of God does not mean that we have to give up a familiar image of God that comforts us. It is good to have many images of God.

No human-created image unveils God.

[Iona Community founder, George] MacLeod
saw creation as 'resplendent'.
He described the air of the eternal
as 'seeping through the physical'.
'What a wonderful world it is,' he said,
'provided you believe in another world.
Not over against this world,
but interlaced with it.'

Listening for the Heartbeat of God
A Celtic Spirituality
by J. Philip Newell[2]

60

Six days later, Jesus took with him Peter and James and his brother John and led them up a high mountain, by themselves. And [Jesus] was transfigured before them, and his face shone like the sun, and his clothes became dazzling white. Suddenly there appeared to them Moses and Elijah, talking with [Jesus].

Then Peter said to Jesus, 'Lord, it is good for us to be here; if you wish, I will make three dwellings here, one for you, one for Moses, and one for Elijah.'

While he was still speaking, suddenly a bright cloud overshadowed them; and from the cloud a voice said,

'This is my Son, the Beloved; with him I am well pleased; listen to him!'

When the disciples heard this, they fell to the ground and were overcome by fear. But Jesus came and touched them, saying, 'Get up and do not be afraid.' And when they looked up, they saw no one except Jesus himself alone.

As they were coming down the mountain, Jesus ordered them, 'Tell no one about the vision until after the Son of Man has been raised from the dead.'

Matthew 17:1–9

In spring, the Mississippi River valley where I live comes to life. The amazingly deep violet blue petals of the scilla, the bright yellow of daffodils, the delicate sweet scent of the plum blossoms, the heady perfume of the lilac, and the familiar song of the wren all bring to mind that poem by Elizabeth Barrett Browning:

> *How do I love thee? Let me count the ways.*
> *I love thee to the depth and breadth and height …*

Could not this amazing diversity of creation and the variety of our seasons be an expression of God's love? As Creator of our universe, God seems to say, 'How do I love? Let me show the many and varied ways …' God shows infinite love through the slow unfurling of tree and flower buds in spring, the verdant heaviness of storms in summer, the harvest colours and pungent smells of autumn, and the pristine beauty of evergreen boughs and naked brown trees draped with white snow in winter.

When I was a freshman in university, there were no more treatments left to put my 16-year-old brother's cancer in remission. He had lived for 13 years with leukaemia. As I packed to return to university after Christmas break, Mom told me to come home every weekend, as he did not have much time left. It was a long, dark winter. He died in February 1979.

That spring, early one morning, I could see something in the weeds, the unmowed area of grass beyond our backyard, but I could not make out what it was. I went out to investigate. The squirrels loved to bury walnuts from our black walnut trees in Mom's flower garden. One of my brother's tasks had been to dig up the little walnut trees and transplant them in the weeds.

I walked into the long grass pressed to the ground from the winter's snow. And there, next to one of the little walnut trees that my brother had planted that last fall, were three yellow tulip buds.

Like the disciples who witnessed the transfiguration of Jesus and the voice of God from the cloud, I did not leap with joy. When the veil between God and our world parts, that revelation can shock, terrify, or reduce us to silence, confusion, babbling. We may experience fear, numbness, awe, amazement or tears.

Peter, James and John were no exception when they witnessed the transfiguration. Just beneath the surface of Jesus's teachings and ministry, they encountered God. How do we honour such moments? Do we realise at that moment that we have just encountered God? Or does it take us a day? Or fifteen years later, does the memory resurface and we realise that *'the air of the eternal'* had seeped through?

Creation does not define God. Creation points us toward God. *'What a wonderful world it is,'* George MacLeod said, *'provided you believe in another world. Not over against this world, but interlaced with it.'*

Nurture life.

We should also realise that the source of our discomfort
is not third world Christians trying to put us down.
It is not they who are giving us a bad time;
rather, the Bible is giving us a bad time.
[Third world Christians] have not created
a new biblical message to make us feel guilty;
they are only calling attention
to the old biblical message we have camouflaged
for centuries in order not to feel guilty.
In ancient times a king would sometimes kill the messenger
who brought bad news – which showed that the king had failed
to locate the source of his problem
and also led to a high absentee rate among messengers
in time of crisis.
No need to perpetuate the king's mistake today.

62

Unexpected News
Reading the Bible with Third World Eyes
by Robert McAfee Brown [3]

And Mary said,

'I'm bursting with God-news;
I'm dancing the song of my Saviour God.
God took one good look at me, and look what happened –
I'm the most fortunate woman on earth!

What God has done for me will never be forgotten,
the God whose very name is holy,
set apart from all others.

His mercy flows in wave after wave
on those who are in awe before him.
He bared his arm and showed his strength,
scattered the bluffing braggarts.
He knocked tyrants off their high horses,
pulled victims out of the mud.

The starving poor sat down to a banquet;
the callous rich were left out in the cold.
He embraced his chosen child, Israel;
he remembered and piled on the mercies,
piled them high.

It's exactly what he promised,
beginning with Abraham and right up to now.'

Luke 1:46–55

How would our faith be changed if our Bible only had Paul's letters but no gospels? On the other hand, how would our faith be changed if our Bible only had the gospels but no letters from Paul?

Paul never met Jesus, who was crucified around 30 AD. In fact, until he too became a follower of Christ, Paul persecuted Christian Jews. Paul wrote his letters during 50–61 AD. The gospels were not written until Mark's around 70 AD, then Matthew and Luke around 80 AD and finally the gospel of John around 100 AD.

If we can acknowledge how different our Christianity would be if we only had Paul's letters or if we only had the gospels, why can we not acknowledge that our brothers and sisters who live in Africa or South America have a valid point of view as they interpret the Bible? Different eyes and different lives see the story of faith differently. Just as Paul understood faith differently as a Jewish man who became a Christian Jew after encountering the risen Christ, so too Jesus's disciples understood Jesus and his mission differently because they knew the Jewish man named Jesus.

As we think about the effect our parents, our country and the era of our birth has on our lives and our faith, we know that Joseph and Mary shaped Jesus's faith. Joseph, a Jewish carpenter of the first century, heeded his dreams, saw angels and listened to them. Mary, a young Jewish woman, also saw an angel, questioned the angel, and then submitted herself to the announcement that she would become pregnant and bear God's son.

In submitting to God, Mary acknowledged victory over injustice in the same manner as prophets before her had done. She did not submit herself to human-made structures. In her greeting to her cousin Elizabeth, she spoke the hymn of praise recorded in the Gospel of Luke, often called 'The Magnificat'. It is similar to the song sung by Hannah, mother of the prophet Samuel (1 Samuel 2:1–10) around 1200 BC.

Mary's song is also similar to the perspective of the Bible pointed out by Africans, Central and South Americans and people from other countries. '[God] *bared his arm and showed his strength, scattered the bluffing braggarts. He knocked tyrants off their high horses, pulled victims out of the mud. The starving poor sat down to a banquet; the callous rich were left out in the cold.'* They point out a God who sides with the poor, with the outcast rather than those who place their faith and base their lifestyle on their wealth and power.

Just as God is unimaginable mystery, so too none of us can proclaim to have a total grasp and understanding of the Bible. We cannot camouflage the Bible's message by saying that our interpretation is the only true interpretation. That would be idolising our own perspective of faith.

God frees us from slavery. Honour the Living God.

The growth of civil society
is already having a major impact
on the way that the international instruments
of the Washington Consensus are conducting their business.
They know they are now being observed.
They know they can no longer take decisions
and expect to implement them in obscurity.
Since Seattle, it has become increasingly difficult
for the meetings of the G8, the WTO
and the World Bank/IMF axis
to take place at all.
Street protests have forced them to convene in places
where they can be insulated by a wide cordon sanitaire
from the rest of the world.
They still display a lot of bravado about all this
– in particular

blaming small violent elements within the protest meetings –
but it is very clear that they and the police protecting them
are extremely rattled.
They can no longer behave like a small exclusive club
entitled to do their business in private.

It Doesn't Have to Be Like This
Global Economics: A New Way Forward
by Margaret Legum [4]

[Jesus] put before them another parable:

'The kingdom of heaven is like a mustard seed that someone
took and sowed in his field; it is the smallest of all the seeds, but
when it has grown it is the greatest of shrubs and becomes a tree,
so that the birds of the air come and makes nests in its branches.'

He told them another parable:

'The kingdom of heaven is like yeast that a woman took and
mixed in with three measures of flour until all of it was leavened.'

Matthew 13:31–33

It generally takes a community of people to bring about change to systems and structures that are already in place. First, we need to be aware of what is happening around us and then pinpoint what we do not like, where it is we disagree.

The G8 is the group of eight countries which represent the major industrialised nations of the world: United Kingdom, United States, France, Germany, Italy, Japan, Canada and Russia. The G8 often works with the World Trade Organization, the World Bank and the International Monetary Fund. All of these international organisations can sound intimidating to an individual. Where does one even begin to make an impact if there is a flaw within the system that perpetuates injustice to nations who are in debt?

What are the primary goals of our nations? Do we wish to be known as citizens rather than consumers? Do we wish to place primary value on relationships rather than money? Once we are aware of our values and know what we like or do not like about a particular system, we need to move from thoughts within our heads to conversations with friends and colleagues. When we share our discontent and our questions among friends or colleagues, we can find out if we are way off base or if others also have discontent and questions.

In July 2005, the G8 met in Scotland. Prior to their meeting, many civic groups in the United Kingdom and other places around the world gathered in Edinburgh to lift up their voices to stand against injustice and poverty. In solidarity with brothers and sisters who live in poverty, around 250,000 peaceful demonstrators rallied.

A person can feel discouraged taking on institutional structures and systems alone. An individual does not feel able to make a huge impact on our international organisations. Yet, as Jesus says in today's passage, *'The kingdom of heaven is like a mustard seed that someone took and sowed in his field; it is the smallest of all the seeds, but when it has grown it is the greatest of shrubs and becomes a tree, so that the birds of the air come and make nests in its branches.'*

We can start taking notice and voicing our analyses of the structures of our world. What a wonderful sense of camaraderie and encouragement there is, when we meet with people who share the same concerns as we do. What joy to meet and share with the people whom we seek to support.

Control greed.

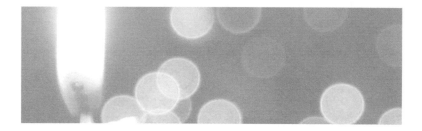

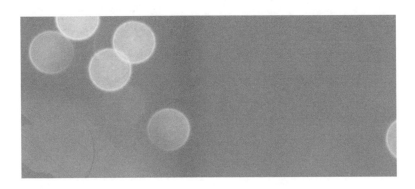

68

And we're here today to say to the leaders of the G8 countries
that we don't think that the right to fair and equal treatment
begins and ends at national borders …
It's a human right,
and poverty in the midst of affluence and privilege
is a violation of human rights.
This is a fantastic show of international solidarity
with people all over the world,
in every continent, but particularly in Africa,
who are working ceaselessly to raise themselves out of poverty
and have to do it with their hands tied behind their backs.
Because let's not be under any illusion
that this event today is about charity,

or doing good to unfortunate people
who happen to be worse off than us,
or have suffered some accident of fate.
There's no accident here.
People live in dire poverty and want
because the political and economic decisions of governments
and international institutions
put them there and keep them there.
This isn't about charity,
this is about justice.

From the Holy City
by Kathy Galloway [5]

When he finally arrives, blazing in beauty and all his angels
with him, the Son of Man will take his place on his glorious
throne. Then all the nations will be arranged before him and he
will sort the people out, much as a shepherd sorts out sheep and
goats, putting sheep to his right and goats to his left.

Then the King will say to those on his right, 'Enter, you who
are blessed by my Father! Take what's coming to you in this
kingdom. It's been ready for you since the world's foundation.
And here's why:

'I was hungry and you fed me, I was thirsty and you gave me a drink, I was homeless and you gave me a room, I was shivering and you gave me clothes, I was sick and you stopped to visit, I was in prison and you came to me.'

Then those 'sheep' are going to say, 'Master, what are you talking about? When did we ever see you hungry and feed you, thirsty and give you a drink? And when did we ever see you sick or in prison and come to you?' Then the King will say, 'I'm telling the solemn truth: Whenever you did one of these things to someone overlooked or ignored, that was me – you did it to me.'

Then he will turn to the 'goats', the ones on his left, and say, 'Get out, worthless goats! You're good for nothing but the fires of hell. And why? Because – I was hungry and you gave me no meal, I was thirsty and you gave me no drink, I was homeless and you gave me no bed, I was shivering and you gave me no clothes, sick and in prison, and you never visited.'

Then those 'goats' are going to say, 'Master, what are you talking about? When did we ever see you hungry or thirsty or homeless or shivering or sick or in prison and didn't help?'

He will answer them, 'I'm telling the solemn truth: Whenever you failed to do one of these things to someone who was being overlooked or ignored, that was me – you failed to do it to me.'

Matthew 25:31–45

The cue word we often miss in this biblical text is 'nations'. We often assume that this story is about individuals being saved. But it clearly says *'all the nations'* will be sorted into sheep and goats by the Son of Man, the king. The sheep go into God's kingdom but the goats go to the fires of hell.

What is interesting about this passage is that neither the sheep nor the goats understand why they are considered faithful or unfaithful. Neither has a clue and they ask why they have been judged the way they have. Through this story, Jesus tells us that it is the way the nations behave that determines how they are judged.

There is nothing about professing faith. There is no requirement that we claim Christ as Lord and Saviour. In this judgement story, believers are not separated from non-believers. Instead, nations that act compassionately for the ignored and neglected people are separated from nations that either have no compassion or do not act upon their compassion.

The issue becomes the use or abuse of power. Power is gained through having money, a certain status or reputation, the use of military force, or being an officer in government or religion. How do our governments use their power?

If we use our power to feed our greed and desires, we are goats. If we use our power for the good of the whole, seeking to eliminate injustice, we are sheep. As many of the prophets of the Bible wrote, the faithfulness of the powerful will be measured by how abundantly they provide for the poor, the widow, and the helpless. Who are the ignored and neglected people in our world today?

After the tsunami struck the countries on the rim of the Indian Ocean in December 2004 and Hurricane Katrina caused flooding of the Deep South in the United States in August 2005, television cameras vividly showed the faces of those left behind by the destruction. We saw how slowly governments moved to provide help. Drawn in percentages, comparisons showed how little money our wealthy, technologically advanced nations spent in recovery and rebuilding and how much we will spend on ourselves.

It was a time of truth-telling for the world as we saw who was assisted and who was ignored. We learned that the natural habitat provided by nature to cushion the Indian Ocean Rim countries from tsunamis had been destroyed for the sake of profit and having a view. We saw the effect of laws enacted and monies not delegated to upgrade the safety of the levees in New Orleans. Out of the ignorance and arrogance of wealthy western nations, groups of ethnic people have become vulnerable to natural catastrophes.

We are rich and powerful nations with citizens who have compassion for the less fortunate. Can more of us move beyond silence or busyness in order to work with people who live in poverty or those who have experienced a natural disaster? The Community of God is in the midst of it all.

Honour the possessions and resources of others.

The priority agenda for Jesus,
and for many of us,
is not mortality or anxiety,
but unrighteousness, injustice.
The need is not for consolation or acceptance
but for a new order
in which men may live together in love.
In [Jesus's] time, therefore, as in ours,
the question of revolution,
the judgement of God upon the present order
and the imminent promise of another one,
is the language in which the gospel must speak.

The Original Revolution
Essays on Christian Pacifism
by John H. Yoder[6]

You have heard that it was said,
'An eye for an eye and a tooth for a tooth.'

But I say to you,
Do not resist an evildoer.

But if anyone strikes you on the right cheek, turn the other also;
and if anyone wants to sue you and take your coat, give your
cloak as well; and if anyone forces you to go one mile, go also the
second mile. Give to everyone who begs from you, and do not
refuse anyone who wants to borrow from you.

You have heard that it was said
'You shall love your neighbour and hate your enemy.'

But I say to you,
Love your enemies and pray for those who persecute you, so that
you may be children of your Father in heaven; for he makes his
sun rise on the evil and the good, and sends rain on the righteous
and on the unrighteous.

For if you love those who love you, what reward do you have?
Do not even the tax collectors do the same? And if you greet only
your brothers and sisters, what more are you doing than others?
Do not even the Gentiles do the same?

Be perfect, therefore, as your heavenly Father is perfect.

Matthew 5:38–48

Yoder writes, *'The need is not for consolation or acceptance but for a new order in which men may live together in love.'* That thought resonates. The image of God as Father has been an image of comfort. Do we need comfort? We have comfort. What most of us need is challenge. God as Creator, as Source of Life in the universe, challenges us to be the best partner with God we are able to be.

Many of us understand the scripture reading for today as promoting a passive acceptance of aggressive, hostile behaviour directed towards us. Matthew 5 begins with the Beatitudes. One of the things Jesus says in the Beatitudes is *'Blessed are the meek for they will inherit the earth.'* (Matthew 5:5) Our passage for today seems to repeat what is said in this Beatitude.

If we lift up just that one verse from the Beatitudes, without being attentive to the other verses, we domesticate and tame Jesus's words. Certainly, we should not be arrogant, but how will God's Community come into the world if we let aggressive, hostile behaviour rule the day?

Was Jesus meek? He had many 'woes' to tell the Pharisees. He turned over the moneychangers' tables in the Temple square. He accused the Sadducees of turning the Temple into a shopping mall. He accused Peter of seeing things the devil's way, not God's way. Jesus was not always meek. In the Beatitudes, Jesus also stated, *'Blessed are those who hunger and thirst for righteousness for they will be filled. Blessed are the peacemakers, for they will be called the children of God. Blessed are those who are persecuted for righteousness'*

sake, for theirs is the kingdom of heaven.' (Matthew 5:6, 9–10)

Again, the English version gives us some trouble. According to Walter Wink, the phrase *'Do not resist an evildoer'* (Matthew 5:39) more accurately translates from the original Greek as *'Don't react violently against the one who is evil.'*[7] But, if we look closely at the English translation following this verse, we can see another attitude besides meekness.

'If anyone strikes you on the right cheek ...' Can a person be hit by a fist on the right cheek? Only if the person hitting is left-handed, otherwise the back of the hand is used, which is an act to humiliate an inferior person. When Jesus adds, *'... turn the other also'* he is encouraging the person being hit to act as if they have equal status. As Wink wrote, *'Jesus is not telling us not to resist evil, but only not to resist it violently.'*[8]

Good Christians are not called to be 'nice', but to be compassionate like Jesus. We do a disservice to Jesus, and therefore God, if we think that we are to let violence have sway on earth without resisting it. Let us not use God's name to promote obedience to situations that sustain evil.

Encourage faithful living by using God's name rightly.

We agreed on two things:
firstly that life was not all about getting what we wanted
or doing what we liked.

And then he, a Muslim,
and I, a Christian,
agreed that one of the purposes of the great world religions
was to enable people to face up to what they would rather avoid.

The more I have mused on that,
the more I am convinced that in the dominant hedonistic culture
which is ours to adopt or transform,
spirituality has precisely that high calling and function.

States of Bliss and Yearning
The Marks and Means of Authentic Christian Spirituality
by John L. Bell[9]

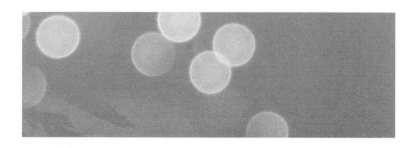

Alas for those who lie on beds of ivory,
and lounge on their couches,
and eat lambs from the flock,
and calves from the stall;

who sing idle songs to the sound of the harp,
and like David improvise on instruments of music;
who drink wine from bowls,
and anoint themselves with the finest oils,
but are not grieved over the ruin of Joseph!

Hear this, you that trample on the needy,
and bring to ruin the poor of the land,
saying, 'When will the new moon be over
so that we may sell grain;
and the Sabbath, so that we may offer wheat for sale?
We will make the ephah small and the shekel great,
and practise deceit with false balances,

buying the poor for silver
and the needy for a pair of sandals,
and selling the sweepings of the wheat.

Amos 6:4–6, 8:4–6

How do we resist the *'dominant hedonistic culture'* which would have us seek only our own pleasure, fulfil our own desires, allow us to wallow without guilt in the greed of wanting more? Bell suggests that that is the task of spirituality. Through faith, we can transform our culture.

In Amos, we have a prophet trying to shake awareness awake in those who had adopted the dominant culture of that time. He spoke to a complacent, satisfied people who had leisure time and who had bought into the injustice of their structures. The people of the northern kingdom of Israel did not wish either to see the poor or heed their needs.

What will we do? Will we adopt or transform the 21st-century culture of our economically and technologically advanced nations? Are we awake enough that we can analyse and critique the structures that underpin our way of life? Are we alert enough to tease out the fine nuances of attitudes that would allow us to slip into a state of sleepiness? It is only if we are awake and alert that we will be able to transform our culture.

Misuse of power weighs heavily when God judges the wealthy. God always sides with the vulnerable. All we need do is look at the stories in the Bible: the story of Moses and the Israelite people living in slavery, the story of Ruth living as a foreigner in Israel, and the story of the Ninevites repenting of their wickedness in the book of Jonah. In the gospels, Jesus healed many of the vulnerable: the little girl who died, the blind man, the haemorrhaging woman, the leper, and so many more.

God takes the side of the vulnerable and judges those who misuse their wealth.

We cannot escape God. We cannot escape God's judgement. *'Your proud heart has deceived you, you that live in the clefts of the rock, whose dwelling is in the heights. You say in your heart, "Who will bring me down to the ground?" Though you soar aloft like the eagle, though your nest is set among the stars, from there I will bring you down, says the Lord'*. (Obadiah 3–4) We cannot escape God no matter where we live. *'Ah, soiled, defined, oppressing city! It has listened to no voice; it has accepted no correction. It has not trusted in the Lord; it has not drawn near to its God.'* (Zephaniah 3:1).

Perhaps we do not wish to escape God and that is why there are all these books today about spirituality as we seek for a better way to understand how to serve God. The prophets of the Bible and the prophets of our world today bring us words of judgement, yet they also bring us words of hope. *'He has told you, O mortal, what is good; and what does the Lord require of you but to do justice, and to love kindness, and to walk humbly with your God?'* (Micah 6:8).

Now is the time to face the reality of a dominant culture that has become self-seeking. There are already groups of people who resist avoidance, who seek awareness and truth. May we join one another in searching for a richer relationship with God through Christ by becoming partners with our neighbours, near and far.

Be a true witness for your neighbour.

FOURTH WEEK
OF ADVENT

GIFTS

If the ruach *is associated with God,
and God with the* ruach,

then

Yahweh's ruach
and Yahweh's dabar★ *– his word –
are very close to one another.*

Ruach *is thought of
as the breath of God's voice.*

The Spirit of Life
A Universal Affirmation
by Jurgen Moltmann[1]

★*whereas* ruach *is feminine,* dabar *is masculine*

Bless the Radiant One, O my soul!
O Heart of my heart, You are so very great!

You are clothed with justice and mercy, arrayed in Light as your fine attire. You stretch over the heavens like a tent, your Radiance covering the waters; You shine through the clouds and ride on the wings of the wind; the wind, like the Breath of Life, carries your Word, fire refines the dross of our souls.

You set the earth on its foundations, strong and secure. You covered it with the deep like a garment, with many waters that life might come forth. At your Word the waters divided, becoming rivers and lakes and mighty oceans; storms came to ensure the balance and to renew the earth. The mountains rose, the valleys became low in the places that You did appoint. You brought harmony to all the earth, that life might spring forth in abundance.

You created springs to flow into the valleys; they flow between the hills, giving drink to every creature of the field, quenching their thirst as your Living Water quenches ours. With the air, You have given birds their habitation; they sing among the branches.

79

The majesty of Creation is seen throughout the land, the sounds of Creation mingle with the music of the spheres.

Psalm 104:1–13 [2]

Creation Story

set to Pachelbel's Canon in D (spoken or sung)

Voice Eternal,
to face of the deep, sing!
Arrangement reveal,
creation, from void, springs.

Burst forth the light, darkness uncreated
Energetic white, melody enlightened.

Dome celestial, separate, waters breach, form assign
Azure order, tempo great, emancipate design.

Briny blue swells, cries, falls free
Transformed, renew, ecstasy!

White mountain peaks, force exultant
Green valleys deep beckon, enchant.

Soil, light, earth shape, reunite, consummate
Grow tall trees, mushrooms, grass and flowers bright-hued.

'Look!' said Sky, 'Blend the elements of air with water,
mould and cast it into a sphere of molten yellow.'

Then said Light, 'I will give of myself to impart life,
burning within this new image in Sky.'

Stretch Light to a soft, white place to govern the night.
Boundaries dynamic allow us to touch.
Voice Eternal unveils and orchestrates the changes.
Ancient patterns can bind us to actions static.

Stars, illuminating, brightly twinkle
glow with velvet splendour.
Hear the night sky,
'Ah!' sighs the Darkness, 'Love, beauty, courage.
Pain can mask much from our hope and vision.'

Come, salty serene
cobalt blue ocean
Whales, dolphins, seahorse
whisper and frolic
Clear cascadences
crest to fresh movement
Walleye, trout, bass, carp …
Water slowing …

Birds are flying through the air,
eagles gliding higher, higher,

hummingbirds sip nectar.

Beasts creep, walk, pounce, run, hop, swing,
snake, elephant, lion, deer, rabbit, monkey.
Is there anything left?

Yes, let's make a person reflect our diversity,
wisdom for discernment, voice, voice to praise all.

Exists the seed within each new being
eternal and deep. Multiply yourselves, sing!

Blessed be all delivered from the womb.
Song of Voice Eternal, gift of structure, time, room.

Listen. What is happening? To this island of time?
In the midst of the eternal now? Listen …

Just as an infant
comes to know his mother
through form and colour,
scent and sound,
so we come to a knowledge of God
through the universe.

Listening to the Heartbeat of God
A Celtic Spirituality
by J. Philip Newell[3]

Through your Word, grass came forth for the cattle, and plants for us to cultivate, that we might have food from the earth, and wine, the fruit of the vine, oil and healing herbs of many varieties, and bread, our daily sustenance. The trees are watered abundantly and, with the sun, provide the air we breathe.

Every living creature has its home: the birds nest in trees, the wild goats upon the mountaintop; even the rocks provide protection.

You created the moon to mark the tides and seasons, the sun, that rises and sets in beauty. In the darkness, when night comes, the creatures of the forest roam the earth. They eat their fill, each according to their need; You provide their food. When the sun rises, they disappear from sight and lie down in their dens. As your people go forth to their work, You are there to guide them.

O You, who know all hearts, how manifold are your works! In wisdom You have created them all; the earth is filled with your creatures. We look to the seas, great and wide, which teem with life innumerable, helping to maintain the balance. O, that we might receive your gifts, taking only what is needed with grateful hearts.

All of creation looks to You, to give them food in due season.

Psalm 104:14–27[4]

Will my children remember me someday in the future when they chop up garlic and onions to sauté in olive oil, the foundation for many of our meals? Will they remember sitting around our dining room table, sometimes in comfortable silence, sometimes using sharp words, sometimes in laughter, chattering about what had happened at school that day?

Smells, sights, sounds and texture bring memories that tell us about relationships. What parts of creation are we most intimate with that can teach us about God? Such a wide variety exists. What do any of these geographical areas and their cycle of seasons teach us about God: the Mississippi River valley in the US, the deserts of Saudi Arabia, the highlands of Scotland, the rainforests of Brazil, the savannahs of Africa, the mountains of India and Tibet, the outback of Australia? What smells, sights and sounds are associated with each of these landscapes, as well as others not listed here?

God comes to us in many guises. We need time and space to reflect and think about how God contacts us through the piece of earth with which we are most familiar. In this age of communication and technology, time and space seem to be a privilege for the wealthy or upper-class citizen but are not available for the working poor. Yet time in nature is important, for many of us find God through creation.

Is there a childhood place in nature that we return to in our dreams or daydreams? What made that place sacred? Do we have a spot in our garden or yard or a public park, where we enjoy spending time now as an adult? What draws us to that place? Do we understand God differently when we are back in our home or workplace and our mind wanders back to our time out in creation?

Think of the smells and the light associated with our sacred place in creation. Do we see it in the light of the rising sun, or the heat of noon, or through a twilight glow or under the stars and moon? Is the air crisp and sharp or is it thick and sultry? Are the colours bright and vibrant or dull and muted? Or, because of the light conditions, do we see it in black and white? Recall the noises that belong in that place, and the textures.

Just as we cannot own God, so too we cannot truly own creation. Creation is a gift bestowed upon us by the grace of God. Out of God has come all of this diversity. What do we learn of our God from our earth, from the galaxy? As the Psalmist wrote, *'O, that we might receive your gifts, taking only what is needed with grateful hearts.'*

In the Hebrew Bible,

which Christians typically call the Old Testament

and which was sacred Scripture

for Jesus and his Jewish contemporaries,

the word compassion *has rich semantic associations.*

In Hebrew (as well as in Aramaic),

the word usually translated as 'compassion'

is the plural of a noun that in its singular form means 'womb'.

In the Hebrew Bible,

84 *compassion is both a feeling*

and a way of being that flows out of that feeling.

Meeting Jesus Again for the First Time:
The Historical Jesus & the Heart of Contemporary Faith
by Marcus J. Borg

When we are in harmony with You,

the earth provides;

yes, a bountiful harvest

to be shared with all.

When we misuse

what You have created for us,

we blame You

for the famine and destruction that ensues,

and feel alienated from You.

Even so,

You continue to send forth your Spirit,

and the earth,

though not without turmoil,

is renewed.

Psalm 104:28–30[6]

I was driving back home after spending the day with my parents. My children were young and had fallen asleep in the car. It was late winter and I drove toward a setting sun over shallow rolling hills. Reflecting on my life at that point in time, having been through a bit of counselling and starting to see my parents, my childhood and my short marriage through different eyes, all of a sudden I heard a voice in my head say, *'For I have brought you up out of the land of Egypt …'* (Exodus 20:2)

That is the beauty of knowing the stories of the Bible. They speak back to us. And as the stories speak back to us, we find a God of compassion, a God who would nourish, a God who would break us free from our misperceptions, from our addictions, from our slaveries.

Today's Psalm reiterates the not-perfectly-remembered passage above, speaking of the turmoil we may go through before being renewed. *'When we misuse what You have created for us, we blame You for the famine and destruction that ensues, and feel alienated from You. Even so, You continue to send forth your Spirit, and the earth, though not without turmoil, is renewed.'* Whether it is famine and destruction of the earth, or a marriage, mental health issues, addictions, or a faulty perception of the world, God will send forth the Spirit to renew us.

In his letter to the people of Corinth, Greece, the apostle Paul alludes to that process. *'When I was a child, I spoke like a child, I thought like a child, I reasoned like a child; when I became an adult, I put an end to childish ways. For now we see in a mirror, dimly, but then we will see face to face. Now I know only in part, then I will know fully, even as I have been fully known.'* (1 Corinthians 13:11–12)

It does not matter what age we are when we start learning the stories of the Bible. If we learn the stories as children, we need to continue learning as adults because there are so many wonderful layers, such as discovering that the Hebrew word for compassion is the plural of the word for a woman's womb.

Once we integrate the stories of the Bible so that they are a part of the memory of our hearts, these faith stories will speak to us during odd moments in our lives. That is the gift given to us.

Our ancient ancestors of faith passed the stories on to the next generation by word of mouth, adding more as they saw God moving and speaking in their present moment. Later ancestors printed the stories of faith but not everyone could read and, until the printing press was invented in the 1500s, there were not a lot of complete Bibles in existence. These ancestors passed on our faith stories through imagination and art – stained-glass windows, carvings on outdoor Celtic crosses, illuminated manuscripts, drama and music.

May we find a vibrant faith through the stories of the Bible and continue to pass on this gift so that our faith stories will speak to the next generation. And may we add our own stories of faith as God moves in our lives.

Gift Economy
is the practice of stepping out of the dominant economy
where money is the basis of exchange,
and stepping into the economy where people share
the gifts of their lives
in ways where the gift continues to move
from person to person,
household to household,
and community to community.

86

People freely give
of their skill, passion, time, and interest.
People put their trust
in relationships rather than in the market economy.
Creation is the best example of Gift Economy.
Air, water, soil, grace, and blessings are given in abundance,
not because we deserve them or 'earn' them –
but because God is the originator and practitioner
of Gift Economy.

Journey into Freedom
by Dale Stitt and Esther Armstrong[7]

The glory of the Radiant One
endures forever,
for the works of Love are sure.

You are ever-present to us,
even as the earth trembles,
even as the mountains spew forth ashes and smoke!

I will abandon myself into your hands as long as I live;
I will sing praise to You while I have breath.

May my meditations be pleasing to You,
for I rejoice and am glad in You.
May all who feel separated from You
open their hearts to new Life!

Praise the Creator of the Universe!
Bless the Heart of my heart,
O my soul!
Amen.

Psalm 104:31–35[8]

Over the past three Wednesdays, we have waded through some daunting words and concepts: economics, neo-liberal capitalism, WTO, World Bank, IMF, structural adjustment, the G8 and civil society. These are systems created by humanity, intended to structure how we share our various resources and gifts. The intent behind these systems may have been noble but, being human-made, they have their flaws. Over time, we discover the flaws that do not lead us toward our values.

Do we place a priority on making a profit for ourselves, our corporations, our nations? Or will we place our highest value on right relationships, building community, preserving creation for the next generation? If we earn a living at the expense of other people, is it worth it? Do we need a totally different economic system? Or do we just need to tweak a few areas in the current economic system?

A gift economy sounds like a lovely dream where people give of *'their skill, passion, time and interest'* and *'put their trust in relationships'*. Is it a realistic dream? If God is the *'originator and practitioner of Gift Economy'* then, since we have been created in the image of God according to Genesis, it is possible.

Perhaps we allow neo-liberal capitalism to be our economic structure because of our overwhelming desire to be secure and safe no matter what the cost. Perhaps we are fearful that, if we do not tightly clutch our money or hang on to what we own, we might become homeless.

Our current economic model is grounded in a lack of trust in the basic goodness of the world and in the intrinsic altruism of humanity. This is the same as saying that we lack trust in God.

Perhaps this lack of trust stems from our separation of spirit from body. When we consider the spirit rather than the body as our gift from God, we figure God will provide for our spirits while we had best provide for our bodies because we mistakenly believe that they are not blessed. Our lack of trust and our need to be in complete control denies the goodness of God's gifts.

What would the world look like if we were to open our fists and let go of our desire to be completely secure? What would our world look like if we opened our minds to the uncommon thought that creation has within it the *'essential goodness of God'* and we reached out an open hand to grasp another person's hand to form community? Our world would change drastically if we did as the Psalmist writes: *'I will abandon myself into your hands as long as I live.'*

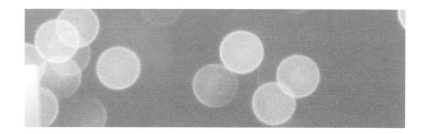

Traditional state and party politics involves winning power
in order to implement your political programme.
This is how most people still understand politics today.
But many indigenous movements have
alternative cultural understandings of power
that do not fit easily into the nation-state structures.
So indigenous movements –
such as in Mexico, the Zapatistas from Chiapas
and groups from Oaxaca,
and in Ecuador, Pachakutik –
are not just taking over existing power structures,
but transforming existing notions
of how power itself should be wielded.
Their view of power is built from the grassroots upwards –
that is, it is embedded in the community.

A Flower in the Hands of the People
What Lies at the Heart of Indigenous Politics in Mexico
by Gustavo Esteva [9]

As Jesus passed along the Sea of Galilee, he saw Simon and
his brother Andrew casting a net into the sea – for they were
fishermen.

And Jesus said to them, 'Follow me and I will make you fish
for people.' And immediately they left their nets and followed him.

As [Jesus] went a little farther, he saw James son of Zebedee
and his brother John, who were in their boat mending the nets.
Immediately he called them; and they left their father Zebedee in
the boat with the hired men, and followed [Jesus].

Mark 1:16–20

William Willimon comments eloquently on this passage from scripture: *'After his dramatic baptism, Jesus strides forth to recapture enemy territory. At last! God is going to get back what belongs to God. The revolution begins today! And what is the first thing Jesus does? What is his first dramatic, decisive act of revolutionary reclamation? He sees a couple of guys mending their nets beside the sea. He says to them, "Follow me!"'* [10]

Jesus called ordinary people to be his disciples. Reading the Gospel of Mark as a whole, we cannot help but be amazed at the extent to which the twelve disciples Jesus chose are not perfect, not powerful, not with it. They seem like the most bumbling, motley group of followers it was Jesus's misfortune to pick!

Yet Jesus knew what he was doing. Jesus knew what he wanted. He did not want to overthrow the Roman government in an act of violence. He did not want his group of disciples to take the rule of the nation in their own hands. The Community of God is not the same as our traditional understanding of a government by the people.

Esteva writes further in his article: *'The old regime is dead but another has not taken its place. The political classes would like to reduce the transition to the simple transfer of state power from one political party to another and the perfection of the representative system, in order to consolidate a "neoliberal republic" tied like a caboose to the US engine.*

'Meanwhile we are rebuilding everything from below. Against the spirit of old-style vanguards, we walk at a slower pace. What counts isn't to arrive sooner or first, but to arrive all together and on time.

'What they call "democracy" can only be where the people are. Instead of representation, we want presentation, presence. And that can only exist in political bodies where we can all take part, in our own communities.' [11]

Jesus gathered four fishermen, a tax collector, a learned Greek-speaking man, two Zealots, an Israelite *'in whom there is no deceit'* (John 1:43), a doubter and perhaps two of his own cousins to be his disciples. Let us not forget the various other supporters he had: Mary Magdalene, the siblings – Lazarus, Martha and Mary – of Bethany, the Samaritan woman at the well, the leper, Jairus, Nicodemus and many more. Out of these assorted individuals, Jesus created community. He ate with them, healed them, told parables, modelled hope, and taught that the Community of God was at hand, sending them out to share the good news.

The Old Testament prophets
can easily be conceived of as guerrillas
doing battle with the established powers of their day;
and their thundering, poetic words and images
surely can be read as forms of prayer.

Certainly Jesus was the pre-eminent guerrilla of grace;
he confronted repressive institutions
and liberated captive minds and hearts
with his words and his life.
A prime weapon in his effort was prayer.

Guerrillas of Grace
Prayers for the Battle
by Ted Loder[12]

90

And [Jesus] said to them,

'So I say to you,
Ask, and it will be given you;
search, and you will find;
knock, and the door will be opened for you.

For everyone who asks receives,
and everyone who searches finds,
and for everyone who knocks, the door will be opened.

Is there anyone among you who, if your child asks for a fish,
will give a snake instead of a fish?
Or if the child asks for an egg, will give a scorpion?

If you then, who are evil,
know how to give good gifts to your children,
how much more will the heavenly Father
give the Holy Spirit to those who ask him!'

Luke 11:5a, 9–13

When we think of guerrillas, we think of murder and killing. Perhaps today we might think of a guerrilla as a terrorist. But that's not our understanding of Jesus. Jesus did not kill anyone. He brought people back to life, he preached about the Community of God being at hand, he expressed anger, but he did not kill.

There was definitely conflict between Jesus and the religious authorities. Their understanding of holiness was different. The Pharisees and Sadducees understood holiness-as-separation. They emphasised purity. Jesus knew God wanted compassion, holiness-as-wholeness.

What were Jesus's options when he realised that his understanding of holiness was in conflict with that of the religious authorities? Jesus knew the Sadducees cooperated with the Roman government. He knew the Romans used crucifixion as a legitimate form of structural violence. Public displays of it were intended to deter any protest or resistance.

Jesus had three options:

— *'retreat from his challenge, explaining that matters are getting out of hand.'*
— *'respond in kind, destruction for destruction.'* As Father Beck said during his workshop, Jesus could have become a 'Jedi knight of Star Wars,' a 'Buffy the vampire slayer,' or a 'Rambo Jesus'.
— *'continue his original programme, but at a heightened level.*

In response to the opponents' consolidation of forces, Jesus consolidates his own following. He names twelve "to be with him and to be sent out" ([Mark] 3:14).' [13]

As a 'guerrilla of grace', Jesus used his prayers to God to guide his behaviour. How did Jesus teach us to pray?

Our passage about prayer from Luke ends with the phrase: *'How much more will the heavenly Father give the Holy Spirit to those who ask him!'* In the parallel passage from Matthew, it is expressed like this: *'How much more will your Father in heaven give good things to those who ask him.'* (Matthew 7:11b)

In the creation story from the book of Genesis, we read how the wind or Spirit from God swept upon the waters and God brought new things to life. God did not kill. God created and gave life. In this abundance of diversity, God set limits, placing boundaries in the midst of the waters to separate the sky from the earth and the sea from the land.

In praying for and receiving the gift that God gives to those who ask, Jesus chose the third option of recommitting to his understanding of holiness. Jesus set his boundaries as determined by his relationship with God. The boundaries Jesus drew brought about consequences. Yet the consequences, imposed by the religious leaders and Roman government, did not deter Jesus from what he was called by God to do.

What encouragement Jesus gives us for how we might live our faith lives today!

CHRISTMAS EVE

Among the most familiar Christmas texts is the one in Isaiah:
'The Lord himself will give you a sign.
Behold, a young woman shall conceive and bear a son,
and shall call his name Emmanuel' (Isaiah 7:14).
Less familiar is its context:

Isaiah has been pleading with King Ahaz
to put his trust in God's promise to Israel
rather than in alliances with strong military powers like Syria.
'If you will not believe, you shall not be established,'
Isaiah warns Ahaz (7:9).
Then the prophet tells the fearful king
that God is going to give him a baby as a sign.

A baby.
Isn't that just like God, Ahaz must have thought.
What Ahaz needed,
with Assyria breathing down his neck,
was a good army,
not a baby.

From a God We Hardly Knew
by William Willimon [14]

It's obvious, isn't it?

The place where your treasure is,
is the place you will most want to be, and end up being.

Luke 12:34

94

Who would think that what was needed
to transform and save the earth,
might not be a plan or army
proud in purpose, proved in worth?
Who would think, despite derision
that a child should lead the way?
God surprises earth with heaven
coming here on Christmas Day. [15]

God saw the human desire for security. Instead of giving us a *good army* to make us more secure, God gave us a baby.

Who is less secure than a baby? Who is more vulnerable than a baby? To our question of what would make us safe and secure, God answered with a baby born in human flesh.

During Advent, I have a recurring daydream: I am alone in a cabin in the northwoods. There is running water! But there is no electricity, no television, no MP3, no mobile phone, no iPod, no appointment calendar, no computer. There is only a bed, a table and chairs, food, a fireplace, a piano and a small shelf of board games and a few books. It is dark and snowing heavily. I do not wish to go out and no one can get to me.

I know that this daydream is a reaction to the excessive commercialism of the period between Hallowe'en and Christmas Eve. In our 'advanced' societies, we are treated not as warm, living, unique persons, but as consumers with money or plastic cards in our pockets and purses. That is how our dominant culture values us.

What is it that John the Baptist warns us against as he prepares us for the coming of Christmas? Is our life green and blossoming? Or is our life deadwood?

When white snowfall masks the Minnesota hills across the river, my strongest desire is to slow down, trudge through the snow, watch the eagles catch their breakfast, breathe the crisp air and reflect upon God's place in my life. I want my life centred on God and I want my lifestyle, my attitude, my behaviour to reflect that yearning. If more people sought to be a Community of God, what a different world we would live in.

As a people of faith, we try not only to understand but also to shape our lives and our relationships centred in the Living God. The gift of Christmas is a God who came to us in the flesh, who became incarnate out of great love for the world.

The season is upon us now,
a time for gifts and giving
and as the year draws to its close
I think about my living.

Christmas time when I was young,
the magic and the wonder,
with colours dull and candles dim
and dark my standing under. [16]

NOTES &
BIBLIOGRAPHY

NOTES

Week One

1. Moltmann, Jurgen, *The Spirit of Life: A Universal Affirmation* (Augsburg Fortress Publishers, 1992) p. 40.

2. Moltmann, Jurgen, *The Spirit of Life: A Universal Affirmation* (Augsburg Fortress Publishers, 1992) p. 40–41, 43.

3. From *Listening for the Heartbeat of God: A Celtic Spirituality* by J. Philip Newell, ©1997 Paulist Press, New York, Mahwah, N.J. Used with permission. www.paulistpress.com. p. 25, and ©1997 Society for Promoting Christian Knowledge by permission of SPCK, p. 25.

4. Myers, Ched, 'To Serve and Preserve', *Sojourners Magazine*, (March 2004) p. 38.

5. Peterson, Eugene H., *Living the Message: Daily Meditations with Eugene H. Peterson* (HarperCollins, 1996). Printed with permission of the author, Eugene Peterson, p. 311.

6. Sampson, Abi, 'Finding a Place in the World', *Coracle: The Magazine of the Iona Community*, (February 2004) p. 13.

7. Sampson, Abi, 'Finding a Place in the World', *Coracle: The Magazine of the Iona Community*, (February 2004) p. 13.

8. From: www.en.wikipedia.org/wiki/World_Trade_Organization, June 28, 2006

9. Pickard, Miguel, 'Introduction to the World Trade Organization' *CIEPAC Centro de Investigaciones Económicas y Políticas de Acción Comunitaria*, © July 2003, p. 1.

10. Pickard, Miguel, 'Introduction to the World Trade Organization' *CIEPAC Centro de Investigaciones Económicas y Políticas de Acción Comunitaria*, © July 2003, p. 1.

11. Brown, Robert McAfee, *Unexpected News: Reading the Bible with Third World Eyes* (Westminster John Knox Press, 1984) p. 50.

12. Borg, Marcus J., *Meeting Jesus Again for the First Time: The Historical Jesus & the Heart of Contemporary Faith,* p. 47 ©1994. Reprinted by permission of HarperCollins Publishers.

13. From *The Abuse of Power: A Theological Problem* by James Newton Poling, ©1991 Abingdon Press, p. 27.

14. Beck, Robert R., *Nonviolent Story: Narrative Conflict Resolution in the Gospel of Mark* (Orbis Books, 1996) p. 88.

Week Two

1. Johnson, Elizabeth A., *She Who Is: The Mystery of God in Feminist Theological Discourse* (Crossroad Publishing Company, 1992) p. 85.

2. Johnson, Elizabeth A., *She Who Is: The Mystery of God in Feminist Theological Discourse* (Crossroad Publishing Company, 1992) p. 264.

3. From *Listening for the Heartbeat of God: A Celtic Spirituality* by J. Philip Newell, ©1997 Paulist Press, New York, Mahwah, N.J. Used with permission. www.paulistpress.com. p. 36, and ©1997 Society for Promoting Christian Knowledge by permission of SPCK. p. 36.

4. From *Listening for the Heartbeat of God: A Celtic Spirituality* by J. Philip Newell, ©1997 Paulist Press, New York, Mahwah, N.J. Used with permission. www.paulistpress.com. p. 35, and ©1997 Society for Promoting Christian Knowledge by permission of SPCK, p. 35.

5. Peterson, Eugene H., *Living the Message: Daily Meditations with Eugene H. Peterson* (HarperCollins, 1996). Printed with permission of the author, Eugene Peterson, p. 297.

6. Legum, Margaret, *It Doesn't Have to Be Like This: Global Economics: A New Way Forward* (Wild Goose Publications, 2002) p. 25.

7. Legum, Margaret, *It Doesn't Have to Be Like This: Global Economics: A New Way Forward* (Wild Goose Publications, 2002) p. 21.

8. Legum, Margaret, *It Doesn't Have to Be Like This: Global Economics: A New Way Forward* (Wild Goose Publications, 2002) p. 32.

9. John L. Bell, *States of Bliss & Yearning: The Marks and Means of Authentic Christian Spirituality* (Wild Goose Publications, Glasgow, 1998) p.65.

10. Beck, Robert R., *Nonviolent Story: Narrative Conflict Resolution in the Gospel of Mark* (Orbis Books, 1996) p. 57.

11. Peters, Arno, *The Peters World Atlas: The Earth in Its True Proportion* ©2002, Peters Atlas, Oxford Cartographers, from the Foreword.

Week Three

1. Johnson, Elizabeth A., *She Who Is: The Mystery of God in Feminist Theological Discourse* (Crossroad Publishing Company, 1992) p. 87.

2. From *Listening for the Heartbeat of God: A Celtic Spirituality* by J. Philip Newell, ©1997 Paulist Press, New York, Mahwah, N.J. Used with permission. www.paulistpress.com. p. 86, and ©1997 Society for Promoting Christian Knowledge by permission of SPCK, p. 86.

3. Brown, Robert McAfee, *Unexpected News: Reading the Bible with Third World Eyes* (Westminster John Knox Press, 1984) p. 158.

4. Legum, Margaret, *It Doesn't Have to Be Like This: Global Economics: A New Way Forward* (Wild Goose Publications, 2002) p. 202.

5. From a speech given by Kathy Galloway on behalf of the Scottish Aid Agencies at the Make Poverty History rally in Edinburgh, 2nd July 2005, subsequently published in 'From the Holy City' *Coracle: The Magazine of the Iona Community* (August 2005) p. 2.

6. From *The Original Revolution* by John Howard Yoder. Copyright © 1971, 1977, 2003 by Herald Press, Scottdale, PA 15683. All rights reserved. Used by permission. p. 18

NOTES

7. Wink, Walter, 'Can Love Save the World?' (Winter 2002) p. 14. Reprinted from *Yes! A Journal of Positive Futures*, PO Box 10818, Bainbridge Island, WA 98110. Subscriptions: 800/937-4451. Web: www.yesmagazine.org.

8. Wink, Walter, 'Can Love Save the World?' (Winter 2002) p. 14. Reprinted from *Yes! A Journal of Positive Futures*, PO Box 10818, Bainbridge Island, WA 98110. Subscriptions: 800/937-4451 Web: www.yesmagazine.org.

9. John L. Bell from *States of Bliss & Yearning: The Marks and Means of Authentic Christian Spirituality* p. 9 (Wild Goose Publications, Glasgow, 1998)

Week Four

1. Moltmann, Jurgen, *The Spirit of Life: A Universal Affirmation* (Augsburg Fortress Publishers, 1992) p. 41.

2. *Psalms for Praying: An Invitation to Wholeness*, Psalm 104, p. 212-214, Nan C. Merrill. ©1996 (2002 edition) Reprinted with permission of the publisher, The Continuum International Publishing Group. Reproduced by kind permission of Continuum International Publishing Group.

3. From *Listening for the Heartbeat of God: A Celtic Spirituality* by J. Philip Newell, ©1997 Paulist Press, New York, Mahwah, N.J. Used with permission. www.paulistpress.com. p. 65, and ©1997 Society for Promoting Christian Knowledge by permission of SPCK.

4. *Psalms for Praying: An Invitation to Wholeness*, Psalm 104, p. 214–215, Nan C. Merrill. ©1996 (2002 edition). Reprinted with permission of the publisher, The Continuum International Publishing Group. Reproduced by kind permission of Continuum International Publishing Group.

5. Borg, Marcus J., *Meeting Jesus Again for the First Time: The Historical Jesus & the Heart of Contemporary Faith,* p.31 ©1994. Reprinted by permission of HarperCollins Publishers.

6. *Psalms for Praying: An Invitation to Wholeness,* Psalm 104, p. 215–216, Nan C. Merrill. © 1996 (2002 edition). Reprinted with permission of the publisher, The Continuum International Publishing Group. Reproduced by kind permission of Continuum International Publishing Group.

7. Written by Esther Elizabeth and published in the 2004 Christmas Letter sent out by Journey Into Freedom (which is no longer in existence). Esther Elizabeth can be reached at 4620 SW Caldew St., Unite E, Portland, OR 97219, USA.

8. *Psalms for Praying: An Invitation to Wholeness*, Psalm 104, p. 216, Nan C. Merrill. ©1996 (2002 edition). Reprinted with permission of the publisher, The Continuum International Publishing Group. Reproduced

NOTES

by kind permission of Continuum International Publishing Group.

9. Esteva, Gustavo, 'A Flower in the Hands of the People', *New Internationalist* (September 2003/Issue 360) p. 20.

10. Esteva, Gustavo, 'A Flower in the Hands of the People', *New Internationalist* (September 2003/Issue 360) p. 21.

11. by William H. Willimon, originally published in *Pulpit Resource,* © Logos Productions, Inc. www.logosproductions.com. Used by permission.

12. Loder, Ted, *Guerrillas of Grace: Prayers for the Battle* © 1984 Innisfree Press used by permission of Augsburg Fortress, p. 7.

13. Beck, Robert R., *Nonviolent Story: Narrative Conflict Resolution in the Gospel of Mark* (Orbis Books, 1996) p. 52.

14. A quote from 'From a God We Hardly Knew', by William Willimon. Copyright 1988 Christian Century. Reprinted by permission from the December 21-28, 1988 issue of *The Christian Century*. Subscriptions: $49/yr. from P.O box 378, Mt. Morris, IL 61054. 1.800.208.4097.

15. 'God's Surprise' (In *Heaven Shall Not Wait*, Wild Goose Publications 1987) Words: John Bell & Graham Maule © 1987, WGRG, Iona Community, Glasgow G2 3DH; US edition © 1987 WGRG/Iona Community. Used by permission of GIA Publications, Inc.

16. *A Baby Just Like You,* Denver, John, and Joe Henry, © 1975 (Renewed) Jesse Belle Denver, Anna Kate Deutschendorf, Zachary Deutschendorf and Cherry Lane Music Inc. All rights on Behalf of Jesse Belle Denver Administered by WB Music Corp. All Rights Reserved. Used by Permission of Alfred Publishing Co., Inc.

16. *A Baby Just Like You,* Words and Music by John Denver and Joe Henry. Copyright © 1975; Renewed 2003 Cherry Lane Music Publishing Company, Inc. (ASCAP), Dimensional Music of 1091 (ASCAP), Anna Kate Deutschendorf, Zachary Deutschendorf and Jesse Belle Denver. All Rights for Dimensional Music of 1091, Anna Kate Deutschendorf and Zachary Deutschendorf. Administered by Cherry Lane Music Publishing Company, Inc. (ASCAP. All Rights for Jesse Belle Denver Administered by WB Music Corp. (ASCAP). International Copyright Secured. All Rights Reserved.

BIBLIOGRAPHY

Beck, Robert, *Nonviolent Story: Narrative Conflict Resolution in the Gospel of Mark,* © 1996, Orbis Books, Walsh Building, PO Box 308, Maryknoll, NY 10545-0308, USA, www.orbisbooks.com

John L. Bell, *States of Bliss & Yearning: the Marks and Means of Authentic Christian Spirituality,* Wild Goose Publications, 4th Floor, Savoy House, 140 Sauchiehall Street, Glasgow G2 3DH, Scotland, www.ionabooks.com

Bell, John and Graham Maule, 'God's Surprise' (In *Heaven Shall Not Wait,* Wild Goose Publications 1987) Words: John Bell & Graham Maule © 1987, WGRG, Iona Community, G2 3DH, Scotland, www.iona.org.uk; US edition GIA Publications, Inc., 7404 South Mason Avenue, Chicago, IL 60638, USA

Borg, Marcus, *Meeting Jesus Again for the First Time: The Historical Jesus & the Heart of Contemporary Faith,* © 1994. Reprinted by permission of HarperCollins Publishers, 10 East 53 Street, New York, NY 10022, USA, www.harpercollins.com

Brown, Robert McAfee, *Unexpected News: Reading the Bible with Third World Eyes,* © 1984. Westminster John Knox Press, 100 Witherspoon Street, Louisville, Kentucky 40202, USA, www.pcc.org

Denver, John, and Joe Henry, *A Baby Just Like You,* Copyright © 1975; Renewed 2003 Cherry Lane Music Publishing Company, Inc. (ASCAP), Dimensional Music of 1091 (ASCAP), Anna Kate Deutschendorf, Zachary Deutschendorf and Jesse Belle Denver. All Rights for Dimensional Music Of 1091, Anna Kate Deutschendorf and Zachary Deutschendorf. Administered by Cherry Lane Music Publishing Company, Inc. (ASCAP). All Rights for Jesse Belle Denver Administered by WB Music Corp. (ASCAP) International Copyright Secured. All Rights Reserved.

Denver, John, and Joe Henry, *A Baby Just Like You,* © 1975 (Renewed) Jesse Belle Denver, Anna Kate Deutschendorf, Zachary Deutschendorf and Cherry Lane Music Inc. All rights on Behalf of Jesse Belle Denver Administered by WB Music Corp. All Rights Reserved. Used by Permission of Alfred Publishing Co., Inc.

Esteva, Gustavo, 'A Flower in the Hands of the People', *New Internationalist,* 55 Rectory Road, Oxford, OX4 1BW, UK, www.newint.org

Elizabeth, Esther, '2004 Christmas letter', *Journey Into Freedom,* (which is no longer in existence). Esther Elizabeth can be reached at 4620 SW Caldew St., Unite E, Portland, OR 97219, USA.

Galloway, Kathy, a speech given on behalf of the Scottish Aid Agencies at the Make Poverty History rally in Edinburgh, 2nd July 2005, subsequently published in *Coracle: The Magazine of the Iona Community,* The Iona Community, 4th Floor, Savoy House, 140 Sauchiehall Street, Glasgow G2 3DH, Scotland, www.iona.org.uk/coracle

BIBLIOGRAPHY

Johnson, Elizabeth A., *She Who Is: The Mystery of God in Feminist Theological Discourse,* Crossroad Publishing Company, 370 Lexington Avenue, New York, NY 10017, USA, www.cpcbooks.com. Reprinted by permission of Copyright Clearance Center.

Legum, Margaret, *It Doesn't Have to Be Like This: Global Economics: A New Way Forward,* Wild Goose Publications, 4th Floor, Savoy House, 140 Sauchiehall Street, Glasgow G2 3DH, Scotland, www.ionabooks.com

Loder, Ted, *Guerrillas of Grace: Prayers for the Battle,* © 1984 Innisfree Press used by permission of Augsburg Fortress, Box 1209, Minneapolis, MN 55440-1209, USA, www.augsburgfortress.org

Merrill, Nan C, *Psalms for Prayer: An Invitation to Wholeness,* Psalm 104, © 1996. Reprinted with the permission of the publisher, The Continuum International Publishing Group, 4775 Linglestown Road, Harrisburg, PA 17112, USA, www.continuumbooks.com

Merrill, Nan C, *Psalms for Prayer: An Invitation to Wholeness,* Psalm 104, © 1996. Reproduced by kind permission of Continuum International Publishing Group, The Tower Building, 11 York Road, London SE1 7NX, England, www.continuumbooks.com

Moltmann, Jurgen, *The Spirit of Life: A Universal Affirmation,* Augsburg Fortress, Box 1209, Minneapolis, Minnesota 55440–1209, USA, www.augsburgfortress.org

Myers, Ched, 'To Serve and Preserve', March 2004 issue of *Sojourners,* 2401 15th Street NW, Washington DC 20009, USA, www.sojo.net

Newell, J. Philip, *Listening for the Heartbeat of God: A Celtic Spirituality,* © 1997 Society for Promoting Christian Knowledge (SPCK), 36 Causton Street, London SW1P 4ST, United Kingdom; US edition Paulist Press, 997 Macarthur Boulevard, Mahwah, New Jersey 07430-2096, USA, www.paulistpress.com

Peters, Arno, *The Peters World Atlas: The Earth in its True Proportions,* Peters Atlas, Oxford Cartographers, 13 Oasis Park, Eynsham, Oxford OX29 4TP, United Kingdom, (44) (0) 1865 882884, info@oxfordcarto.com

Peterson, Eugene, *Living the Message: Daily Meditations with Eugene H. Peterson,* © 1996 HarperCollins (Harper SanFrancisco). Printed with permission of the author, Eugene Peterson.

Pickard, Miguel, *Introduction to the World Trade Organization: FAQ about the WTO,* © July 1993 by Centro de Investigaciones Económicas y Políticas de Acción Comunitaria, Calle de la Primavera No. 6 Barrio de la Merced, 29240 San Cristóbal de Las Casas, Chiapas, Mexico.

Poling, James Newton, *The Abuse of Power: A Theological Problem,* Abingdon Press, 201 Eighth Avenue South, Nashville, TN 37202-0801, USA, www.abingdonpress.com

BIBLIOGRAPHY

Sampson, Abi, 'Finding a Place in the World', *Coracle: The Magazine of the Iona Community*, The Iona Community, 4th Floor, Savoy House, 140 Sauchiehall Street, Glasgow G2 3DH, Scotland, www.iona.org.uk/coracle.

Willimon, William H., *Revolution!* Originally published in *Pulpit Resource,* © Logos Production, Inc. 6160 Carmen Ave, Inver Grove Heights, MN 55076-9910, USA, www.logosproductions.com Used with permission

Willimon, William H., 'From A God We Hardly Knew', Copyright 1988 Christian Century. Reprinted by permission from the December 21-28, 1988 issue of *The Christian Century*. Subscriptions: $49/yr. from P.O. Box 378, Mt. Morris, IL 61054. 1-800-208-4097.

Wink, Walter, 'Can Love Save the World?', *Yes! A Journal of Positive Futures*, PO Box 10818, Bainbridge Island, WA 98110-0818, USA, 1.800.937.4451 www.yesmagazine.org

Yoder, John Howard, *The Original Revolution: Essays on Christian Pacifism*, Mennonite Publishing Network, 616 Walnut Avenue, Scottdale, PA 15683, USA, www.mph.org

BIBLE READING SOURCES

Week/Day	Main quotes	Within reflection
1st Sunday	NRSV [1]	NRSV
Monday	NRSV	NRSV
Tuesday	The Message [2]	NRSV
Wednesday	The Message	
Thursday	The Message	
Friday	The Message	
Saturday	NRSV	
2nd Sunday	NRSV	NRSV
Monday	NRSV	NRSV
Tuesday	NRSV	NRSV
Wednesday	The Message	NRSV
Thursday	NRSV	NRSV
Friday	The Message	NRSV
Saturday	The Message	NRSV
3rd Sunday	NRSV	NRSV
Monday	NRSV	
Tuesday	The Message	
Wednesday	NRSV	
Thursday	The Message	
Friday	NRSV	NRSV
Saturday	NRSV	NRSV

Week/Day	Main quotes	Within reflection
4th Sunday	Psalms for Prayer [3]	
Monday	Psalms for Prayer	
Tuesday	Psalms for Prayer	NRSV
Wednesday	Psalms for Prayer	
Thursday	NRSV	NRSV
Friday	NRSV	NRSV
Saturday	The Message	

[2] Peterson, Eugene, *The Message: The Bible in Contemporary Language* © 1993, 1994, 1995, 1996, 2000, 2001, 2002. Used by permission of NavPress Publishing Group, Colorado Springs, CO, USA.

[3] Merrill, Nan C, *Psalms for Prayer: An Invitation to Wholeness* © 1996. Reprinted with the permission of the publisher, The Continuum International Publishing Group, 4775 Linglestown Road, Harrisburg, PA 17112, USA, www.continuumbooks.com

MORE RESOURCES FOR ADVENT & CHRISTMAS:

Candles & Conifers
Resources from All Saints' to Advent
Ruth Burgess

A collection of seasonal resources for groups and individuals – prayers, liturgies, poems, reflections, sermons, meditations, stories and responses, written by Iona Community members, associates, friends and others. It covers the weeks from All Saints' Day to Christmas Eve, including saints' days, Remembrance Day, World AIDS Day and Advent. There are liturgies for an outdoor celebration with fireworks, a Christingle service and a longest night service, as well as Advent candle ceremonies, personal prayer practices, a series of responses and blessings and a cats' Advent calendar.

ISBN 978-1-901557-96-1

Hay & Stardust
Resources for Christmas to Candlemas
Ruth Burgess

This companion resource book to *Candles & Conifers* covers the season of Christmastide, including Christmas Eve, Holy Innocents' Day, Winter and New Year, Epiphany, Homelessness Sunday and Candlemas. It also contains eight Christmas plays, including a puppet play.

ISBN 978-1-905010-00-4

Hear My Cry
A daily prayer book for Advent
Ruth Burgess

A daily prayer book for Advent which can also be used as a prayer journal, taking its inspiration from the Advent antiphons – a group of prayers that reflect on the character and activities of God. The pages can be added to and personalised, with line drawings that can be coloured in and space to add your own pictures, reflections and prayers. Instructions for three workshops are also included to enable Advent themes to be explored in a group setting.

ISBN 978-1-901557-95-4

The Jesse Tree
Daily readings for Advent
Thom Shuman

We know the familiar stories like Noah and the Ark; we know the famous people, like Mary and David – but what about those people who might only be mentioned once in the Bible (in the lineages in Matthew and Luke)? What about the women, the prophets, the exiles who, while not linked to Jesus genetically, nevertheless passed on their 'spiritual DNA' to him and to us? They are just as much a part of his heritage, his family, his 'tree' as all his relatives by blood and by marriage. They are a part of the tradition and faith we seek to pass onto our children and grandchildren. They are branches on the Jesse tree.

ISBN 978-1-905010-06-6

Innkeepers and Light Sleepers
Seventeen songs for Christmas
Book and CD
John L. Bell

Seventeen songs for Christmas which attempt to convey the earthiness of the people involved in the story as well as expressing the mystery of the incarnation. Includes suggestions as to how each carol may be sung co-operatively, encouraging adventurous sharing. On the CD, all carols are sung by the Wild Goose Worship Group.

Book ISBN 978-0-947988-47-0
CD   ISBN 978-1-901557-39-8

Doing December Differently
An alternative Christmas handbook
Nicola Slee & Rosie Miles

Explores how people of faith and goodwill might mark the midwinter season and the Christmas festival with integrity and simplicity, in ways that include others and celebrate difference, that do not put us all under strain, or perpetuate false and oppressive myths of the ideal family life. Includes historical, theological, liturgical and sociological reflections about the origins, meanings and customs associated with Christmas, as well as liturgical and ritual resources that can be adapted and used in the home, in group gatherings and in church settings.

ISBN 978-1-905010-23-3

Cloth for the Cradle
Worship resources & readings for Advent,
Christmas & Epiphany
Wild Goose Worship Group

Containing a wealth of different types of worship resources: litanies, meditations, monologues, poems, prayers, readings, scripts and symbolic actions. Its prime purpose is to allow the adult world to rediscover the stories of Christ's birth as speaking from and to adult experience. Drawn from the work of the Wild Goose Worship Group, *Cloth for the Cradle*'s range and diversity offers a unique source of elements for lay and clergy worship planners and enablers.

ISBN 978-1-901557-01-5

Advent Readings from Iona
Brian Woodcock & Jan Sutch Pickard

Part of a biblical journey through lectionary passages for the season, linked to the shared experience of work and worship on Iona. Intended to be a book from and for companions – folk sharing bread and sharing a way of life. The authors were Warden and Deputy Warden of The Abbey and MacLeod Centre on the Isle of Iona at time of writing.

ISBN 978-1-901557-33-6

THE IONA COMMUNITY IS:

- An ecumenical movement of men and women from different walks of life and different traditions in the Christian church
- Committed to the gospel of Jesus Christ, and to following where that leads, even into the unknown
- Engaged together, and with people of goodwill across the world, in acting, reflecting and praying for justice, peace and the integrity of creation
- Convinced that the inclusive community we seek must be embodied in the community we practise

Together with our staff, we are responsible for:

- Our islands residential centres of Iona Abbey, the MacLeod Centre on Iona, and Camas Adventure Centre on the Ross of Mull

and in Glasgow:

- The administration of the Community
- Our work with young people
- Our publishing house, Wild Goose Publications
- Our association in the revitalising of worship with the Wild Goose Resource Group

The Iona Community was founded in Glasgow in 1938 by George MacLeod, minister, visionary and prophetic witness for peace, in the context of the poverty and despair of the Depression. Its original task of rebuilding the monastic ruins of Iona Abbey became a sign of hopeful rebuilding of community in Scotland and beyond. Today, we are about 250 Members, mostly in Britain, and 1500 Associate Members, with 1400 Friends worldwide. Together and apart, 'we follow the light we have, and pray for more light'.

For information on the Iona Community contact:
The Iona Community, Fourth Floor, Savoy House, 140 Sauchiehall Street,
Glasgow G2 3DH, UK. Phone: 0141 332 6343
e-mail: admin@iona.org.uk; web: www.iona.org.uk

For enquiries about visiting Iona, please contact:
Iona Abbey, Isle of Iona, Argyll PA76 6SN, UK. Phone: 01681 700404
e-mail: ionacomm@iona.org.uk